Praise fo
Whispei

"Few authors capture the imagination with the written word like Mark Batterson. His personal stories and biblical convictions will lead you to new places as you are encouraged to lean into and listen for the voice of God day after day. Open your heart, but more importantly open your ears and discover afresh the whisper of a God who still longs to speak to His people."

—BRIAN HOUSTON, founder and global senior pastor
of Hillsong Church

"If you've ever longed to hear the voice of God, this book is an essential guide. I've been deeply blessed by the personal and prescriptive words of Mark Batterson in *Whisper*. Packed full of practical steps and godly wisdom, *Whisper* is one of those books you won't be able to put down. It will open your eyes and your ears to God in a new way."

—CHRISTINE CAINE, founder of Propel Women and author
of *Unashamed*

"Some of the most frequent questions I get as a pastor have to do with hearing from God. In *Whisper*, Mark Batterson cuts through the confusion and shows the way to a deeper and closer relationship with God—one that leaves us guessing less and discerning more."

—STEVEN FURTICK, pastor of Elevation Church and *New York Times* bestselling author

"Not a day passes that I don't ask, 'Lord, what should I do?' I need His counsel and crave His guidance. For that reason I welcome this book. May God use it to attune my heart to His."

—MAX LUCADO, pastor and author

WHISPER

WHISPER

How to Hear
the Voice of God

Mark Batterson

MULTNOMAH

WHISPER

Trade Paperback ISBN 978-0-7352-9110-2
Hardcover ISBN 978-0-7352-9108-9
eBook ISBN 978-0-7352-9109-6
Proprietary ISBN 978-0-525-61724-2

Published in the United States by Multnomah, an imprint of Random House, a division of Penguin Random House LLC.

MULTNOMAH® and its mountain colophon are registered trademarks of Penguin Random House LLC.

Originally published in hardcover in the United States by Multnomah, an imprint of Random House, a division of Penguin Random House LLC, in 2017.

The Library of Congress has cataloged the hardcover edition as follows:
Names: Batterson, Mark, author.
Title: Whisper : how to hear the voice of God / Mark Batterson.
Description: First Edition. | Colorado Springs : Multnomah, 2017.
Identifiers: LCCN 2017028952 | ISBN 9780735291089 (hardcover) | ISBN 9780735291096 (electronic)
Subjects: LCSH: Listening—Religious aspects—Christianity. | Spirituality—Christianity. | God
   (Christianity)
Classification: LCC BV4647.L56 B38 2017 | DDC 248—dc23
LC record available at https://lccn.loc.gov/2017028952

Printed in the United States of America

10 9 8 7 6 5 4 3 2 1

Dedicated to Paul McGarvey, a mentor in ministry.
You prayed a prayer in August of 1984 that
God answered on July 2, 2016.

Contents

Prologue: The Tomatis Effect 1

PART ONE: THE POWER OF A WHISPER

1 The Bravest Prayer 7

2 The Voice 19

3 The Whispering Spot 35

PART TWO: THE SEVEN LOVE LANGUAGES

4 Sign Language 53

5 The Key of Keys—Scripture 63

6 The Voice of Gladness—Desires 77

7 The Door to Bithynia—Doors 95

8 Dreamers by Day—Dreams 115

9 Hidden Figures—People 129

10 The Archer's Paradox—Promptings 147

11 Joystick—Pain 169

Epilogue: The Whisper Test 185

Discussion Questions 191

Notes 203

THE TOMATIS EFFECT

Speak, LORD, for your servant is listening.

—1 SAMUEL 3:9

More than half a century ago, Dr. Alfred Tomatis was confronted with the most curious case of his fifty-year career as an otolaryngologist. A renowned opera singer had mysteriously lost his ability to hit certain notes even though those notes were well within his vocal range. He had been to other ear, nose, and throat specialists, all of whom thought it was a vocal problem. Dr. Tomatis thought otherwise.

Using a sonometer, Dr. Tomatis discovered that even an average opera singer produces 140-decibel sound waves at a meter's distance.[1] That's slightly louder than a military jet taking off from an aircraft carrier. And the sound is even louder inside one's skull. That discovery led to a diagnosis: the opera singer had been deafened by the sound of his own voice. Selective muteness was caused by selective deafness. If you can't hear a note, you can't sing that note. In Dr. Tomatis's words, "The voice can only reproduce what the ear can hear."[2]

The French Academy of Medicine dubbed it the Tomatis effect.

I'm guessing you, like me, have your fair share of problems. And your problem-solving techniques might be as effective as mine, which isn't very. Maybe that's because we're treating symptoms while ignoring the root cause: a spiritual Tomatis effect. Is it possible that what we perceive to be relational, emotional, and spiritual problems are actually hearing problems—

ears that have been deafened to the voice of God? And it's that inability to hear His voice that causes us to lose our voice and lose our way.

Let me make a bold statement at the beginning of this book: Learning how to hear the voice of God is the solution to a thousand problems! It's also the key to discovering our destiny and fulfilling our potential.

His voice is love.

His voice is power.

His voice is healing.

His voice is wisdom.

His voice is joy.

If your life is off-key, maybe it's because you've been deafened by the negative self-talk that doesn't let God get a Word in edgewise! Maybe you've listened to the voice of criticism so long you can't believe anything else about yourself. Or maybe it's the Enemy's voice of condemnation that speaks lies about who you really are. If you don't silence those competing voices, they'll eventually deafen you. You won't be able to sing God's song because you won't be able to hear His voice.

Is God's voice the loudest voice in your life?

That's the question.

If the answer is no, that's the problem.

We live in a culture where everyone wants to have his or her voice heard but has so little to say. And that's because we do so little listening, especially to God. The best way to get people to listen to us is for us to listen to God. Why? Because we'll have something to say that is worth hearing.

Ultimately, all of us need to find our voice. And by voice I mean the unique message God wants to speak through our lives. But finding our voice starts with hearing His voice.

Would you be willing to pray a bold prayer at the beginning of this book? It's an ancient prayer. It's a prayer that can change the trajectory of your life, just as it did for a prophet named Samuel. Before you pray it, let me issue one warning. If you aren't willing to listen to *everything* God has to say, you eventually won't hear *anything* He has to say. If you want to hear His comforting voice, you have to listen to His convicting voice. And it's often what we want to hear *least* that we need to hear *most*. Trust me, though, you want to hear what He has to say.

Are you ready?

Here's the seven-word prayer that can change your life:

Speak, LORD, for your servant is listening.[3]

That prayer is easier said than done, no doubt. But if you meant what you just prayed, your life is about to change for the better.

Part One

THE POWER OF A WHISPER

1

THE BRAVEST PRAYER

After the fire came a gentle whisper.

—1 Kings 19:12

On the morning of August 27, 1883, ranchers in Alice Springs, Australia, heard what sounded like gunshots.[1] The same mysterious sound was reported in fifty geographical locations spanning one-thirteenth of the globe. What those Aussies heard was the eruption of a volcano on the remote Indonesian island of Krakatoa 2,233 miles away!

That volcanic eruption, possibly the loudest sound ever measured, was so loud that the 310-decibel sound waves circumnavigated the globe at least four times. It generated three-thousand-foot tidal waves, threw rocks a distance of thirty-four miles, and cracked one-foot-thick concrete three hundred miles away![2]

If you were to drill a hole directly through the center of the earth, opposite of Krakatoa you would find Colombia, South America. Although the sound of the eruption wasn't audible in Colombia, there was a measurable spike in atmospheric pressure because of infrasonic sound waves that caused the air to tense. The sound may not have been *heard*, but it was *felt*, all the way around the world. According to science journalist and *New York Times* columnist Maggie Koerth-Baker, "Just because you can't hear a sound doesn't mean it isn't there."[3]

At low levels sound is imperceptible.

At high levels it's unignorable.

If sound exceeds 110 decibels, we experience a change in blood pressure. At 141 decibels we become nauseous. At 145 decibels our vision blurs because our eyeballs vibrate. At 195 decibels our eardrums are in danger of rupturing. And death by sound waves can happen at 202 decibels.[4]

The act of hearing is detecting vibrations of the eardrum caused by sound waves, and the intensity of those waves is measured in decibels. On one end of the sound spectrum is the sperm whale, the loudest animal on earth. The clicking noise it uses to echolocate can hit 200 decibels. Even more impressive, researchers believe that whale songs may travel up to ten thousand miles underwater![5] Next to the sperm whale is jet engines (150 decibels), air horns (129 decibels), thunderclaps (120 decibels), and jackhammers (100 decibels).[6]

What's on the other end of the sound spectrum?

A whisper, measuring just 15 decibels.

Technically speaking, our absolute threshold of hearing is 0 decibels. That corresponds to a sound wave measuring 0.0000002 pascals, which causes the eardrum to vibrate by just 10^{-8} millimeters. That's less than a billionth of the ambient pressure in the air around us and smaller than the diameter of a hydrogen atom![7]

Juxtapose that with this:

> Then a great and powerful wind tore the mountains apart and
> shattered the rocks before the LORD, but the LORD was not in
> the wind. After the wind there was an earthquake, but the LORD
> was not in the earthquake. After the earthquake came a fire, but
> the LORD was not in the fire. And after the fire came a gentle
> whisper.[8]

The ESV calls it "a low whisper."

The NASB calls it "a gentle blowing."

The KJV calls it "a still small voice."

We tend to dismiss as insignificant the natural phenomena that preceded the whisper because God was not in them, but I bet they got Elijah's attention. God has an outside voice, and He's not afraid to use it. But when God wants to be heard, when what He has to say is too important to miss, He often speaks in a whisper just above the absolute threshold of hearing.

The question, of course, is *why*.

And *how*.

And *when* and *where*.

Those are the questions we'll explore and seek to answer in the pages that follow.

The Sound of Silence

The Hebrew word for "whisper," *demamah*, can be translated "silence" or "stillness" or "calmness."[9] Simon and Garfunkel weren't far off with the title of their 1964 hit single, "The Sound of Silence." The same Hebrew word is used to describe the way God delivers us from our distress: "He stilled the storm to a whisper; the waves of the sea were hushed."[10] And that psalm foreshadows the way Jesus would stop a storm in its tracks with three words: "Quiet! Be still!"[11]

His whisper is gentle, but nothing is more powerful.

My dictionary defines *whisper* as "speaking very softly using one's breath without one's vocal cords." The use of breath instead of vocal cords is significant. Isn't that how God created Adam? He whispered into the dust and named it Adam.

Adam was once a whisper.

So were you.

So was everything else.

Whispering is typically employed for the sake of secrecy. No form of communication is more intimate. And it seems to be God's preferred method.[12] The question again is *why*. And I won't keep you guessing any longer.

When someone speaks in a whisper, you have to get very close to hear. In fact, you have to put your ear near the person's mouth. We lean toward a whisper, and that's what God wants. The goal of hearing the heavenly

Father's voice isn't just hearing His voice; it's intimacy with Him. That's why He speaks in a whisper. He wants to be as close to us as is divinely possible! He loves us, likes us, that much.

When our children were young, I would occasionally play a little trick on them. I'd speak in a whisper so they would inch closer to me. That's when I'd grab them and hug them. God plays the same trick on us. We want to hear what He has to say, but He wants us to know how much He loves us.

"The voice of the Spirit is as gentle as a zephyr," said Oswald Chambers. "So gentle that unless you are living in perfect communion with God, you never hear it."[13] Aren't you grateful for a gentle God? The Almighty could intimidate us with His outside voice, but He woos us with a whisper. And His whisper is the very breath of life.

Chambers continued, "The checks of the Spirit come in the most extraordinarily gentle ways, and if you are not sensitive enough to detect His voice you will quench it, and your personal spiritual life will be impaired. His checks always come as a still small voice, so small that no one but the saint notices them."[14]

Once a Whisper

For the past two decades, I've had the joy and privilege of pastoring National Community Church in Washington, DC, and I wouldn't want to be anyplace else doing anything else with anyone else. I'm living the dream, but that dream was once a whisper.

The genesis of the dream goes all the way back to a cow pasture in Alexandria, Minnesota, where I heard the still small voice of God. I had just finished my freshman year at the University of Chicago, where I was a PERL (politics, economics, rhetoric, and law) major. Law school was Plan A, but that was before I asked God a dangerous question: *What do You want me to do with my life?* Of course, it's far more dangerous *not* to ask Him that question!

In retrospect I've dubbed that summer between my freshman and sophomore years of college my "summer of seeking." For the first time in my life, I got serious about getting up early in the morning to pray. And it wasn't just a religious ritual. I was desperate to hear His voice, and maybe that's why I finally did.

At the end of the summer, our family was vacationing at Lake Ida in Alexandria, Minnesota. I decided to do a long prayer walk down some dirt roads. For some reason walking helps my talking. I'm able to pray with more focus and listen with less distraction. At one point I went off road through a cow pasture. As I meandered my way around cow patties, I heard what I would describe as the inaudible yet unmistakable voice of God. In that moment at that place, I knew that God was calling me into full-time ministry. It wasn't words as much as it was a feeling, a sense of calling. And that one whisper prompted me to give up a full-ride scholarship at the University of Chicago and transfer to Central Bible College in Springfield, Missouri. That move made no academic sense whatsoever and was second-guessed by more than a few people in my life, but that's often the way His whisper works.

Those who dance are thought mad by those who hear not the music.

That old adage is certainly true of those who walk to the beat of God's drum. When you take your cues from the Holy Spirit, you'll do some things that will make people think you're crazy. So be it. Obey the whisper and see what God does.

More than two decades of ministry have come and gone since that prayer walk through a cow pasture. National Community has grown into one church with eight campuses over the past twenty years, but each campus was once a whisper. I've written fifteen books over the past ten years, but each book was once a whisper. Every sermon I preach and every book I write are echoes of that one whisper in the middle of a cow pasture in the middle of nowhere.

Nothing has the potential to change your life like the whisper of God. Nothing will determine your destiny more than your ability to hear His still small voice.

That's how you discern the good, pleasing, and perfect will of God.

That's how you see and seize divine appointments.
That's how God-sized dreams are birthed.
That's how miracles happen.

The Bravest Prayer

There are days, and then there are days that alter every day thereafter. For me, one of those life-altering days is July 2, 2016. Next to the day I was married, the days my kids were born, and the day I almost died, no day is more sacred. In fact, I can tell you exactly how many days it's been from that day to this day.

I was kicking off a series of sermons titled "Mountains Move" and challenged our church to pray the bravest prayer they could pray. By bravest prayer I mean the prayer you can barely believe God for because it seems impossible. It's often the prayer you've prayed a hundred times that hasn't been answered, but you pray it one more time anyway. For me the bravest prayer was that He would heal my asthma. And it was brave because asthma is all I had ever known.

My very first childhood memory is of a middle-of-the-night asthma attack followed by a frantic trip to the emergency room for a shot of epinephrine. That routine was repeated more times than I can remember. There weren't forty days in forty years that I did not need to take a puff of my albuterol inhaler, and I never went anywhere without it. Never ever. Then I prayed my bravest prayer, and I haven't taken a single puff of an inhaler from that day to this day. That's why I literally count the days, because each day is more miraculous than the last.

Over the span of forty years, I must have prayed hundreds of times that God would heal my asthma. But for reasons known only to Him, those prayers went unanswered.

Why did I keep praying?

The short answer is one whisper.

Right before my freshman year of high school, I was hospitalized for a severe asthma attack that landed me in the intensive care unit. It was one of a dozen such hospitalizations during my younger years. When I was released from Edward's Hospital a week later, Pastor Paul McGarvey and a prayer team from Calvary Church in Naperville, Illinois, came over to our house, laid hands on me, and prayed that God would heal my asthma.

God answered that prayer for healing but not in the way I expected.

When I woke up the next morning, I still had asthma, but all the warts on my feet had mysteriously disappeared. I'm not kidding! At first I wondered if God had made a mistake. Maybe the signals between here and heaven were mixed. I couldn't help but wonder if someone somewhere was breathing great but still had warts on his or her feet. I was a little confused, but that's when I heard the still small voice. It wasn't an audible voice; it was Spirit to spirit. And it was loud and clear: *Mark, I just wanted you to know that I'm able!*

All these decades later it still sends a chill down my spine. I was fourteen years old, and it was the first time I heard God's whisper. Was I disappointed that He hadn't answered my prayer the way I wanted Him to? Of course I was. But those two words echoed for three decades: *I'm able.* And He's not just able; He's "able to do immeasurably more than all we ask or imagine, according to his power that is at work within us."[15]

Let me connect the dots.

Without that whisper I'm not sure I would have had the faith to pray the bravest prayer. And if I hadn't prayed that prayer, how could God answer it? After all, God doesn't answer 100 percent of the prayers we don't pray! You can guess where this is going, can't you? My miracle was once a whisper. And that's true of every miracle. As I survey my life, I realize that the genesis of every blessing, every breakthrough is the breath of God. It started out as nothing more than a still small voice.

Ebenezers, the coffeehouse on Capitol Hill that our church owns and operates, is a perfect example. When people walk by Ebenezers, they see a coffeehouse, but when I walk by it, I hear a whisper. That's all it was two decades ago. Actually, it was a graffiti-covered building with cinder blocks in the doorframes. Then one day I walked by and a Spirit-inspired thought fired across my synapses: *This crack house would make a great coffeehouse.*

That thought came out of nowhere, which sometimes indicates some-thing supernatural. I call it a God idea, and I'd rather have one God idea than a thousand good ideas. Good ideas are good, but God ideas change the course of history.

That God idea turned into a brave prayer, which turned into a coffee-house that has been voted the number-one coffeehouse in DC more than once. Since opening the doors a decade ago, we've given more than a million dollars to kingdom causes from its net profits. But every shot we pull and every dollar we give was once a whisper.

The Think Tank of the Soul

For the past thirty-plus years, an acoustic ecologist named Gordon Hempton has compiled what he calls "The List of the Last Great Quiet Places." It consists of places with at least fifteen minutes of uninterrupted quiet during daylight hours. At last count there were only twelve quiet places in the entire United States![16] And we wonder why the soul suffers. As Hempton noted, "Quiet is a think tank of the soul."[17]

Simply put, God often speaks loudest when we're quietest.

Seventeenth-century French philosopher Blaise Pascal once observed, "The sole cause of man's unhappiness is that he does not know how to stay quietly in his room."[18]

That's quite a statement, but it's not an overstatement. If our problems are hearing problems—the spiritual Tomatis effect—then the solution to those problems is a prescription that is as old as the psalms. It's so critical to our spiritual vitality that it's worth meditating on one word or phrase at a time:

Be.
Be still.
Be still, and know.
Be still, and know that I am God.[19]

Have you ever tried to quiet a loud room? Attempting to yell above the crowd usually doesn't work, does it? It's far more effective to shush the crowd with a *shhh*. That's the method God employs. His whisper quiets us, calms us, stills us.

By definition, white noise is a sound that contains every frequency a human can hear.[20] And because it contains every frequency, it's very difficult to hear any frequency, especially the still small voice of God. As such, chronic noise may be the greatest impediment to our spiritual growth. And it's not just spirituality that suffers.

In a study of elementary-age students at a grade school in Manhattan, psychologist Arlene Bronzaft found that children assigned to classrooms on the side of the school facing the elevated train tracks were eleven months behind their counterparts on the quieter side of the building. After New York City Transit installed noise-abatement equipment on the tracks, a follow-up study found no difference between the groups.[21]

When our lives get loud, with noise filling every frequency, we lose our sense of being. We run the risk of turning into human doings rather than human beings. And when our schedules get busy, we lose our sense of balance, which is a function of the inner ear.

Can I go out on a limb?

Your life is too loud.

Your schedule is too busy.

That's how and why and when we forget that God is God. And it takes very little to distract us. "I neglect God and his angels, for the noise of a fly," said the English poet John Donne.[22] The solution? Stillness. Or more specifically, His still small voice.

Silence is anything but passive waiting. It's proactive listening. The noted author and professor Henri Nouwen believed that silence was an act of war against the competing voices within us. And that war isn't easily won, because it's a daily battle. But each day God's voice gets a little louder in our lives until He's all we can hear. "Every time you listen with great attentiveness to the voice that calls you the Beloved," said Nouwen, "you will discover within yourself a desire to hear that voice longer and more deeply."[23]

Songs of Deliverance

Over the past decade I've recorded a dozen audiobooks with a brilliant sound engineer named Brad Smiley. During our last recording session, Brad told me about standard operating procedure for sound mixers in the film and music industries. Before going into the studio, they let their ears relax and recalibrate through absolute silence. Only then are they ready to listen, really listen. Acoustic ecologists call the process ear cleaning.

The quietest room in the world is the anechoic chamber at Orfield Laboratories in Minneapolis. One-foot-thick concrete walls and three-foot-thick fiberglass acoustic wedges absorb 99.99 percent of sound. Background noise measures –9.4 decibels.[24] All you hear in an anechoic chamber is the sound of your heart beating, blood circulating, and lungs breathing. That's the sound of silence, and it reminds us that it's in God that "we live and move and have our being."[25]

If you want to hear the heart of God, silence is key.

If you want the Spirit of God to fill you, be still.

The psalmists didn't have an anechoic chamber to retreat to, so they retreated to God. They referred to Him as their refuge, their fortress, and their ever-present help in time of need. They spoke of the "shelter of the Most High" and the "shadow of the Almighty."[26] But my favorite descriptor might be the "hiding place."

> You are my hiding place;
> you will protect me from trouble
> and surround me with songs of deliverance.[27]

Did you know that God is singing songs of deliverance all around you all the time? You can't hear them because they're outside your range of hearing, but you're surrounded by a sonic shield. Those songs of deliverance are powerful enough to break any bondage, overcome any addiction, and solve any problem. Those songs are the reason no weapon formed against you will prosper.[28]

Remember, the voice can reproduce only what the ear can hear. I'm not sure what problem you need to solve or what issue you need to resolve, but my prayer is that you'll learn to discern His voice. When you do, His songs of deliverance can set you free!

Quit hiding *from* God.

Hide yourself *in* Him.

An Eighth Rest

One of the most played pieces of classical music is Beethoven's *Symphony No. 5* in C minor. It's immediately recognizable because of its iconic opening, a four-note motif that is among the most famous in Western music. But did you know that it actually begins with silence? Beethoven inserted an eighth rest before the first note.[29]

Beethoven's Fifth is so familiar to us that it's difficult to re-create the full effect it had when it debuted at Vienna's Theater an der Wien on December 22, 1808. And although it's difficult to discern Beethoven's original intent, that eighth rest served as a sonic buffer. At the beginning of a concert there is ambient noise: conversations between concertgoers, a few stragglers finding their seats, the rustling of programs. A bit of silence at the beginning of a symphony is ear cleaning, even if it's only an eighth rest. It was silence that set up that symphony, and the same is true of our lives.

We need more eighth rests, don't we? Especially if we want our lives to be symphonies of God's grace. I would recommend an eighth rest at the beginning and end of the day—a few moments to collect our thoughts, count our blessings, and pray our prayers. We also need a day of rest one day a week. Rest is so important that the Sabbath is one of God's Ten Commandments. And if you can afford the time, I would recommend a two-day silent retreat once a year. In my opinion you can't afford not to. Make sure you tell someone where you're going and how long you'll be gone, but cut off all communication for two days. Get alone with God and His Word. And although prayer is an important part of a silent retreat, do more listening than talking.

Remember those voices that deafen us? It's hard to tune them out and turn them down, especially the voices in our heads. But the payoff is exponential: "Better is one day in [the Lord's] courts than a thousand elsewhere."[30] If we want to do more by doing less, we need to get into God's presence. It's our most efficient use of time, by a factor of a thousand. And quiet is the key. It's silence that helps us hear God's voice and sing His song.

Silence is the difference between sight and insight.

Silence is the difference between happiness and joy.

Silence is the difference between fear and faith.

According to interruption science, we're interrupted every three minutes.[31] And the very fact that we have a field of science dedicated to interruption is evidence of how bad it's gotten. To find peace and quiet, we need to set some boundaries. For example, no e-mail before nine o'clock in the morning or after nine at night. And while we're setting boundaries, we might want to delete a few apps, cancel some subscriptions, and take a break from social media every now and then.

A few years ago I wrote a book titled *The Circle Maker*.[32] It's about the power of prayer, and the thousands of testimonies I've heard since the book was released is evidence to that fact. Prayer is the difference between the best we can do and the best God can do. But there is something even more important and powerful than *talking* to God. What is it? *Listening* to God. It turns a monologue into a dialogue, which is exactly what He wants.

I have a simple rule of thumb when I meet with someone: do more listening than talking. The more I want to hear what the person has to say, the quieter I am. That's a good rule of thumb with God.

Lean into His whisper.

Then pray the bravest prayer!

2

THE VOICE

God said, "Let there be light."

—GENESIS 1:3

You may have no sensation of motion right now, but that is an illusion of miraculous proportions. The reality? You are on a planet that is spinning around its axis at a speed of approximately 1,000 miles per hour. And you don't even get a little bit dizzy! Plus, planet Earth is speeding through space at approximately 67,000 miles per hour. So even on a day when you feel as if you didn't get much done, you traveled 1,608,000,000 miles through space!

Now let me ask: When was the last time you thanked God for keeping us in orbit? I'm guessing the answer is *never*. Why? Because God is so good at what He does that we take it for granted. Never once have I knelt and prayed, *Lord, I wasn't sure we'd make the full rotation today, but You did it again.*

There are people, and perhaps you are one of them, who would say they've never experienced a miracle. With all due respect, I beg to differ. We experience a miracle of astronomical proportions each and every day. The irony is that we already trust God for the big miracles, like keeping us in orbit. Now the trick is trusting Him for the little miracles: everything else.

In order to fully appreciate the power of God's voice, we have to go all the way back to the beginning. He speaks the universe into existence with, count them, four words:

God said, "Let there be light."[1]

Here's a paraphrase:

Let there be electromagnetic radiation with varying wavelengths traveling at 186,282 miles per second. Let there be radio waves, microwaves, and X-rays. Let there be photosynthesis and fiber optics. Let there be LASIK surgery, satellite communication, and suntans. Oh, and let there be rainbows after rainstorms.

"Let there be light."

These are God's first recorded words.

This is God's first recorded miracle.

Light is the source of *vision;* without it we can't see a thing. Light is the key to *technology;* it's how we can talk to someone halfway around the world without so much as a second's delay because light can circle the globe seven and a half times a second.[2] Light is the first link in the *food chain;* no photosynthesis equals no food. Light is the basis of *health;* the absence of light causes everything from vitamin D deficiency to depression. Light is the origin of *energy;* in Einstein's equation $E = MC^2$, energy (E) is defined as mass (M) times the speed of light (C) squared. The speed of light is the constant. And light is the measuring stick for *space-time;* a meter is defined as the distance traveled by light in a vacuum during a time interval of 1/299,792,458 of a second.

Light is the alpha and omega of everything, and that includes you.[3]

Did you know that embryologists have recently captured the moment of conception via fluorescence microscopy? What they discovered is that at the exact moment a sperm penetrates an egg, the egg releases billions of zinc atoms that emit light.[4] Sparks fly, literally! That miracle of conception is a microcosm that mirrors God's first four words.

Four Words

On January 1, 1925, Edwin Hubble gave a presentation to the American Astronomical Society that proved to be a cosmological paradigm shift.[5] At the time, the prevailing opinion was that the Milky Way galaxy might be the sum total of the cosmos. Hubble, a pioneer in extragalactic astronomy, argued otherwise. His key piece of evidence was the degree of redshift observed in light coming from distant stars that increased in proportion to their distance from planet Earth. In one fell swoop the size of the known universe was increased by a factor of one hundred thousand. Even more significant was this simple fact: the universe is still expanding. Nearly a century later the Hubble telescope has spied an estimated two hundred billion galaxies, and recent research indicates that this estimate may be at least ten times too low.[6]

Here is the significance of that discovery: the four words spoken by God in the beginning are still creating galaxies at the outer edges of the universe. Four words! And the result is an ever-expanding universe that measures at least ninety-three billion light-years in diameter.[7]

If God can do that with four words, what are we worried about?

The very first revelation of God was as Creator. And because His creation is so awe inspiring, it's easy to overlook *how* God did what He did. But to me, the mechanism of creation is just as amazing as creation itself.

How did God create? With His voice! The universe is His way of saying, "Look at what I can do with four words." The voice that spoke the universe into existence is the same voice that parted the Red Sea and made the sun stand still. His voice can heal a withered hand or wither a barren fig tree. His voice can turn water into wine, install synaptic connections between the optic nerve and visual cortex in a blind man's brain, and resurrect a man four days dead.[8]

There is nothing God's voice cannot say, cannot do. And, frankly, He can do it however He pleases! He can speak through burning bushes, Balaam's donkey, or Bethlehem's star. His voice can write on palace walls or shut the mouths of lions. It can quench the flames of a fiery furnace or stop a storm on the Sea of Galilee.[9]

The voice of God is all-powerful, but that's only half the story. His voice is also all-loving. In the pages that follow, we'll explore seven languages of God. The first language is Scripture, and it's the Rosetta stone. The other six languages we'll look at are secondary languages: desires, doors, dreams, promptings, people, and pain. But all of them are love languages. Why? Because "God is love."[10]

Sweetness

One reason we turn a deaf ear to God is because we're afraid of what He's going to say, but that's because we don't know His heart toward us. You want to hear what He has to say. Trust me. The Song of Songs says, "His mouth is sweetness itself."[11]

According to rabbinic tradition, when God spoke to the Israelites at Mount Sinai, they were so scared that they felt as though their souls left them.[12] That's what happens when God uses His outside voice! So what did God do? He sweetened His words, softened them, until their souls returned to them.[13] Maybe that is nothing more than a rabbinic legend, but it fits God's character. When He wants us to repent, what does He do? He doesn't threaten us or nag us or yell at us. He shows us kindness.[14] And if that doesn't work? He resorts to more kindness.

For eighteen months Zac Jury attended National Community Church while working at FBI headquarters. Zac is your prototypical agent. He's a tough guy, a smart guy. But all of us have a soft spot, and that is often where God speaks to us.

"I never really understood or really accepted that God loves me for me, as me," said Zac. "But that changed the day I stood at the end of an NCC service at the Lincoln Theatre—row J, seat 111. That's where I heard the still small voice say over and over again, *I love you, I love you, I love you, I love you, I love you, I love you.* He must have whispered those words to me at least a hundred times. With tears pouring down my face, I experienced His love in the most visceral way I ever have. The Lincoln Theatre is a profoundly special place to me. It will forever be the place where I heard, really heard and believed, that the Lord loves me."

I believe that if you listen carefully, you'll hear the same thing.

I know that many people have a hard time believing God is loving, and it's often because someone represented Him in a way that *misrepresented* Him. But I promise you this: the heavenly Father is speaking over us the same thing He spoke over Jesus at His baptism: "This is my beloved Son, in whom I am well pleased."[15] You are His beloved, and He's especially fond of you. You just have to let Him love you.

Isn't that a voice you want to hear?

During our dating days Lora and I attended different colleges for a semester. As I have already mentioned, I eventually transferred from the University of Chicago to Central Bible College. But it wasn't just because I felt a call to ministry. It was also because the phone calls were going to cost more than tuition. It was cheaper to transfer.

Why did we spend hours on the phone during those long-distance days? Because when you love someone, you love the sound of his or her voice. And you long to hear it. A relationship with God is no different.

And God Sang

The famed composer and conductor Leonard Bernstein believed that "the best translation of the Hebrew in Genesis 1 was not 'and God said' but 'and God sang.'"[16] Although there might be a musical prejudice at play, I quite like his interpretation. Creation is God's symphony, and science provides plenty of corroborating evidence.

Did you know that the electron shell of the carbon atom produces the same harmonic scale as the Gregorian chant?[17] Makes you go *hmmm*.

According to the science of bioacoustics, millions of songs are being sung all the time. Of course, the vast majority of those songs are infrasonic and ultrasonic. "If we had better hearing," said physician and researcher Lewis Thomas, "and could discern the descants of sea birds, the rhythmic timpani of schools of mollusks, or even the distant harmonics of midges hanging over meadows in the sun, the combined sound might lift us off our feet."[18]

Juxtapose that with this.

Then I heard every creature in heaven and on earth and under the earth and in the sea. They sang:

"Blessing and honor and glory and power
    belong to the one sitting on the throne
    and to the Lamb forever and ever."[19]

This isn't future-tense prophecy; it's present-tense reality.

When we cross the space-time continuum and enter a dimension the Bible calls heaven, we'll get a glorified body. And I'm looking forward to some new body parts, including glorified abs! But what excites me most is the thought of glorified senses. We'll finally be able to hear angel octaves, and their chorus will lift us off our feet. Until then, we settle for Bach or Bono or Bieber.

One footnote. Remember Dr. Alfred Tomatis? He said, "The ear has a poor physiological response to pure sounds." Instead, "It loves complexity." What kind of complexity? "In order for the ear to respond tangibly, a minimum of three frequencies must be put into simultaneous play."[20]

Three frequencies? What a coincidence, or perhaps providence!

Creation is three-part harmony: Father, Son, and Holy Spirit. And just as the Trinity sang every atom into existence, every atom echoes its unique note back to God. Creation is call and response. When Scripture speaks of mountains singing and trees clapping, it's not just metaphorical.[21] If our range of hearing were a little better, we would hear the voice of God in every drop of water, every blade of grass, every grain of sand.

Range of Hearing

When we see the word *said,* we think phonics, but we should think physics, especially if God is the One doing the saying. After all, sound is first and foremost a form of energy. The human voice is pretty much good for one thing—verbal communication. So we tend to think of God's voice in the same vein. But His voice is so much more than audible words communicated in human language. God uses His voice to speak, but He also uses it to heal and reveal, convict and create, guide and grace. For His voice to be fully appreciated, it must be compared and contrasted with the human voice.

Scientifically speaking, the human voice is made up of sound waves traveling through space at 1,125 feet per second. The average male speaks at a frequency of 100 hertz, while the average female speaks in a higher-pitched voice, around 150 hertz. There are the Barry Whites and Céline Dions, who push vocal boundaries, but our vocal range is between 55 and 880 hertz. We also have a range of hearing, and it's limited to sound waves between 20 and 20,000 hertz. Anything below 20 hertz is infrasonic. Anything above 20,000 hertz is ultrasonic.[22] And it's when we get outside our range of hearing that the miracle of sound is really revealed.

Below our range of hearing, infrasound has the capacity to cause headaches and earthquakes. According to zoologists, using infrasound is the way elephants predict changes in weather. It also helps birds navigate as they migrate. And infrasound can also be used to locate underground oil or predict volcanic eruptions.

Above our range of hearing, ultrasound has the capacity to kill insects, track submarines, break glass, perform noninvasive surgery, topple buildings, clean jewelry, catalyze chemical reactions, heal damaged tissues, pasteurize milk, break up kidney stones, drill through steel, and give you a glimpse of your unborn baby via sonogram.

Does God speak audibly? Absolutely! But that's a thin slice of His vocal range. His ability to speak is way beyond our ability to hear audibly. Just as there are people who claim they've never experienced a miracle, there are people who argue that they've never heard the voice of God. I would argue otherwise. That may be true of His audible voice within our small range of hearing, but everything we see was structured by His acoustic oscillations.

What we see today, He once said.

His voice is all around us, all the time!

Bigger Than Big

If creation reveals anything, it's that God is bigger than big. The theological word is *transcendence,* and it's evidenced by the size of the universe.

Earth is larger than Mars, Mercury, and the moon. But it's significantly smaller than Uranus, Neptune, Saturn, and Jupiter. Jupiter is 1,321 times larger than Earth in terms of volume, but it's 10 times smaller than the sun. And the sun is a relatively small yellow dwarf star. Arcturus, an orange giant, is 26 times bigger than the sun and produces 200 times more energy. Antares, a red supergiant, is 10,000 times brighter than the sun. And we're not even out of the Milky Way galaxy!

And to us, Earth seems huge. Not so much.

It's not just a reminder of how incredibly small we are; it's a reminder of how incredibly big God is. He doesn't exist within the space-time dimensions that He created, so quit putting four-dimensional limits on Him. "With the Lord a day is like a thousand years, and a thousand years are like a day."[23] That makes no sense if you exist in a time dimension, but it makes perfect sense if you exist outside of time.

We have a hard time thinking of God in anything other than four dimensions, because that's all we've ever known. And we try to create God in our image rather than allowing Him to create us in His. What we end up with is a god, lowercase *g,* who walks and talks an awful lot like us.

"How much happier you would be," said G. K. Chesterton, "how much more of you there would be, if the hammer of a higher God could smash your small cosmos!"[24]

God is bigger than big, but that's a little intimidating if left by its lone-some. The good news? There is a theological counterbalance to that bigness. It's called the immanence of God: God is also closer than close.

> God's love is meteoric,
>   his loyalty astronomic,
> His purpose titanic,
>   his verdicts oceanic.
> Yet in his largeness
>   nothing gets lost.[25]

God is great not just because nothing is too big; God is great because nothing is too small. God doesn't just know you by name; He has a unique name for you.[26] And He speaks a language that is unique to you.

Custom Fitted

The twenty-ninth psalm is a powerful yet poetic depiction of God's outside voice. I often think of that psalm during thunderstorms because in it the voice of the Lord is depicted as peals of thunder and flashes of lightning. Then there is this statement, which seems to be an understatement: "The voice of the LORD is powerful."[27]

One translation says, "The voice of the Lord is fitted to the strength."[28] In other words, it is custom fitted to the unique strength of each and every person. Translation: God speaks your language!

There is a theory in organizational development called appreciative inquiry that I subscribe to as a leader and a parent. Instead of exclusively focusing on what's wrong and trying to fix it, you identify what's right and try to replicate it. Appreciative inquiry is playing to people's strengths. It's catching people doing things right. It's celebrating what you want to see more of. And it's bragging about people behind their backs.

I'm certainly not suggesting that God doesn't convict us of our sin; He does. Call it a "sin inquiry" if you want. But He also pulls our potential out of us via appreciative inquiry. Why? Because He's the One who gave it to us in the first place. How? By speaking to our strengths.

In part 2 of this book, we're going to explore seven of God's love languages. But it's not an exhaustive list by any means. I don't even include the language of nature, which seems like a sin of omission. The reality? God speaks billions of dialects, including yours.

I recently met an Indian pediatrician who attends our church and who grew up in a Hindu family. She told me that she put her faith in Jesus Christ while reading a book called *Am I a Hindu?*[29] I don't know if there is another person on the planet who found Jesus the way this woman did. But it's a testament to the God who speaks our unique language.

Lost in Translation

In her brilliant book *A Natural History of the Senses,* author Diane Ackerman humorously shared an incident that reveals how difficult it can be to understand one another, even if we speak the same language. Diane, who hails from Waukegan, Illinois, was visiting Fayetteville, Arkansas, when she asked her host if there was a spa in town. Ackerman was aware of the famous hot springs and thought it would be an enjoyable way to spend the afternoon. She quickly discerned by the quizzical look on her host's face that something got lost in translation. "Spas?" said her host in a thick Arkansan accent. "You mean Russian agents?"[30]

We don't always hear what's actually being said. Why? Because we hear everything through the filter of our histories, our personalities, our ethnicities, and our theologies.

Did you know that citizens of different countries actually hear differently? It's called a basic-frequency band. The French ear, for example, hears best between 1,000 and 2,000 hertz. The British bandwidth is much larger, between 2,000 and 12,000 hertz. And the American ear hears between 750 and 3,000 hertz.[31]

In a very real sense, there is a French ear, a British ear, and an American ear. I might also suggest that there is a Catholic ear and a Protestant ear, a Republican ear and a Democrat ear, a male ear and a female ear. Just because we speak the same language, it doesn't mean we hear one another. We speak dialects that are as different as *spas* and *spies*.

And what's true linguistically is true spiritually. I absolutely believe in absolute truth, but my understanding of that truth is not omniscient. It's not even objective. Thankfully, there is a God who is big enough to speak a language we each can understand.

Big Enough

In his book *A Mile Wide,* Brandon Hatmaker shares the story of his first trip to Ethiopia, when he went to work with his friend Steve Fitch, the founder of Eden Projects. Deforestation has devastated parts of Ethiopia as generation after generation has stripped the forests bare, leaving the land barren. Eden is a reforestation effort, with a vision to plant a hundred million trees.

By the time Brandon boarded the plane, he was having second thoughts about the trip. He had a fear of flying, he was leaving his family behind, and he wondered what difference his going would make. Brandon was feeling bad about his attitude, so he closed his eyes and prayed, "God, I'm sorry. I'm trying, but I just don't get it. I don't want to be on this plane. I feel like I'm wasting time and money. If this is important to you, will you please overcome my ignorance, doubt, and blindness? Will you connect the dots and show me what I'm missing? Amen."[32]

No sooner had Brandon opened his eyes than the thirtysomething Ethiopian man sitting next to him asked why he was going to Ethiopia. Brandon could have given a few different answers, ranging from community development to ministry. For some reason he simply said he was going to plant trees. That's when the elderly woman sitting next to the Ethiopian man asked him a question in Amharic. When he responded in Amharic, she literally began to wail. In fact, she stood up and starting waving her hands in the air like she really did care.

"What's going on?" Brandon asked.

"My mother asked me why you were going to Ethiopia," he said.

Brandon responded, "What did you tell her?"

He said, "I told her you were going to plant trees."

And Brandon asked, "What is she saying?"

That's when Brandon's seatmate revealed that his mother had been praying for thirty-eight years that God would forgive her people for stripping their land. She also had been praying for Him to send someone to plant trees. Before Brandon knew what was happening, this woman was laying her hands on his head and praying for him through her tears of joy.

Can I remind you of a simple truth? You are the answer to someone else's prayer. In this instance it was a prayer that this woman had been praying for longer than Brandon had been alive. And I might add, it was a brave prayer!

Not surprisingly, Brandon had a renewed sense of purpose. And he walked away from that experience with this insight: "My gospel was too small."[33] Maybe it's not just our gospel that is too small. Maybe it's also our understanding of God's voice.

I have a fundamental conviction: God is big enough. He's big enough to keep the planets in orbit. He's big enough to reveal Himself to Babylonian astrologers living a thousand miles from Bethlehem. He's big enough to reveal Himself to Hindu pediatricians and Ethiopian grandmothers. And on a personal note, He's big enough to reveal himself to a five-year-old boy named Mark Batterson through a Billy Graham film called *The Hiding Place*.[34]

God is big enough.

He's big enough to speak through doors and dreams and people.

He's close enough to speak through desires and promptings and pain.

Closer Than Close

Long before the Holy Spirit filled or stirred or gifted or convicted or sealed or revealed or reminded, we find Him hovering over the surface of the deep.[35] And He is still hovering over our lives the way He hovered over creation.

He still speaks light into darkness.

He still brings order out of chaos.

He still makes beauty out of ashes.

The Hebrew word used to describe God's proximity is *paniym,* and it's multidimensional. In regard to time, *paniym* refers to the split second before and the split second after—a parenthesis in time. In regard to space, *paniym* refers to the place right in front and right in back—a parenthesis in space.

He is God *with* us in every sense of the word.

He is a friend that sticks *closer* than a brother!

A. W. Tozer pictured *paniym* this way: "God is above, but He's not pushed up. He's beneath, but He's not pressed down. He's outside, but He's not excluded. He's inside, but He's not confined. God is above all things presiding, beneath all things sustaining, outside of all things embracing and inside of all things filling."[36]

The Holy Spirit is hovering. The Holy Spirit is whispering. The Holy Spirit is breathing into you the same breath He breathed into the dust bowl named Adam.

Remember the bravest prayer that I prayed? For the first few weeks, I wasn't sure whether or not I was healed of my asthma, so I asked God to confirm it somehow, someway. More specifically, I asked Him for a word from His Word, and He gave me just that. I didn't, however, expect it to be *one* word or an Aramaic word: *"Ephphatha!"*[37] It means "Be opened!" and it's the one word Jesus used to heal a man with a speech impediment. Scripture says that when the man's ears were opened, his tongue was untied, and he spoke plainly. Notice the sequence.

Is it possible Jesus knew that speech problems were hearing problems long before Dr. Alfred Tomatis came along? Well, Dr. Tomatis himself cited this miracle of Jesus as the confirmation of his conclusion that the mouth can speak only what the ear can hear.[38]

The focus of this chapter has been on the power of God's voice. God created galaxies with four words! And evidently He can open deaf ears with one word. Just as Jesus opened this man's ears with one word, he opened my lungs. And that word has become one of my favorite words.

Along with asking God for a confirmation of healing, I started researching anything and everything related to respiration. I'm not sure how this theory stayed hidden from me through three seminary degrees, but it has forever changed the way I think about the twenty-three thousand breaths we take every day.[39] Some Hebrew scholars believe that the name of God, Yahweh—or without the vowels, YHWH—is synonymous with the sound of a breath. On one hand, the name is too sacred to pronounce. On the other hand, it's whispered with each and every breath we take. It's our first word, our last word, and every word in between.

God is as close as the breath we breathe.

Catholic priest Desiderius Erasmus coined the Latin phrase *vocatus atque non vocatus, Deus aderit.* Translation: "Bidden or not bidden, God is here." The Swiss psychiatrist Carl Jung engraved those words above the door of his home.[40] Not unlike the Jewish custom of engraving the words of the Shema on the doorposts of one's home, that simple statement served as a constant reminder of God's presence: omnipresence.

Scripture paints the picture of a God who exists outside of time—the One who was, who is, who is to come. It paints the picture of a God who exists outside of space—the One who is here, there, and everywhere.

But there is one place where God finds Himself on the outside looking in, and that place is the door to your heart. If you want to hear His voice, you have to answer the knock.

By Invitation Only

In 1853 English artist William Holman Hunt painted a portrait of Jesus standing at a door and knocking. He called it *The Light of the World,* and it's a visual representation of Revelation 3:20: "I stand at the door and knock. If anyone hears my voice and opens the door, I will come in and eat with that person, and they with me."

Fifty years later Hunt said that it was more than a painting. It was a prompting, a divine command.[41] One fascinating feature of the painting is that the door has no handle on the outside, and it was left off intentionally. Why? Because the door to the heart is opened only from the inside. God enters by invitation only. And that's not just true of Jesus; it's true of the Holy Spirit too.

I recently spoke at a pastors' conference in England. It was my first time speaking to our compatriots across the pond, so I wasn't entirely sure what to expect. I think I was subliminally influenced by the series *Downton Abbey*, thinking the setting might be somewhat formal, somewhat ascetic. But what I encountered was so life giving that I wished I could bottle that experience and uncork it in the church I pastor.

One simple practice left a lasting impression on me, and it's a mainstay in the Anglican tradition. It's the recitation of the simplest of prayers: *Come, Holy Spirit.* The Latin phrase *Veni Creator Spiritus* may have originated with a ninth-century hymn written by a Benedictine monk, Rabanus Maurus. Since the English Reformation in the sixteenth century, there have been more than fifty translations. But the version included in the 1662 revision of *The Book of Common Prayer* is this:

Come, Holy Ghost, our souls inspire,
and lighten with celestial fire.
Thou the anointing Spirit art,
who dost thy sevenfold gifts impart.

This prayer was prayed over King Charles I at his coronation in 1625, and the very same prayer has been prayed at the coronation of every English monarch since. Those words are sung by the coronation choir after the singing of the Creed, while the king or queen is seated in the Coronation Chair, just prior to the anointing.[42]

You don't have to tell the Holy Spirit when or where or how to come, but you should extend an invitation. This prayer is not an "abracadabra."

The danger with any repeated prayer is that it can become an empty incantation. But if you pray it and really mean it, don't be surprised if the Holy Spirit shows up and shows off in some strange and mysterious ways!

And remember, it won't really be God speaking any louder than He already is. It'll be you listening a little closer, a little better.

Maybe this is your bravest prayer?

3

THE WHISPERING SPOT

So is my word that goes out from my mouth.

—Isaiah 55:11

In March of 1792, Secretary of State Thomas Jefferson announced a competition awarding five hundred dollars and a city lot to whoever produced "the most approved plan" for the United States Capitol. None of the seventeen plans submitted were accepted. After the competition closed, a Scottish-trained physician living in the British West Indies, Dr. William Thornton, requested permission to submit a proposal, and his plans were ultimately accepted. The amateur architect became known as the "first architect" and, a decade later, the first superintendent of the United States Patent Office.[1]

The year after Thornton submitted his Capitol plan, President George Washington led a parade of people to Jenkins Hill, now Capitol Hill. With music playing, drums resounding, colors flying, and spectators celebrating, the cornerstone of the Capitol was laid on September 18, 1793. It was consecrated with corn, wine, and oil. And the festivities concluded with a five-hundred-pound ox being butchered, setting a precedent for one of America's most sacred rituals: the barbecue![2]

With two hundred twenty-five years of history under its belt, the Capitol is perhaps the most storied structure in America. The decisions made, actions taken, and conversations had within those hallowed halls have altered the course of history time and time again. If those walls could talk, they would tell of public hearings and private conversations, floor debates and committee votes, that have forged this nation.

It was there, on May 24, 1844, that Samuel Morse tapped the first long-distance telegraph message, "What hath God wrought!" Morse's prototype had sent messages between the House and Senate wings of the Capitol, but those dots and dashes traveled thirty-eight miles to a train depot in Baltimore, Maryland, revolutionizing communication in a way that wouldn't be felt again until the invention of the telephone or the advent of e-mail and the Internet.[3]

It was there, on March 3, 1865, that Abraham Lincoln, while signing end-of-the-session legislation in the president's room, first learned of the South's desire to surrender. The very next day Lincoln delivered his second inaugural address, "with malice toward none; with charity for all," from the East Portico.[4] And six weeks later our sixteenth president was laid in state in the Capitol rotunda, the victim of John Wilkes Booth's .44-caliber bullet.

It was there, on December 8, 1941, that Franklin Delano Roosevelt rallied a grief-stricken nation the day after "a date which will live in infamy."[5] After he delivered that speech to a joint session of Congress, America declared war on Japan for its unprovoked attack on Pearl Harbor and entered the Second World War.

For the past twenty years, I've lived precisely one mile from the Capitol. I can see the Statue of Freedom sitting atop the cast-iron dome from our home. We picnic at the Capitol in the summer and sled there in the winter. Yet despite the fact that I drive by it or run around it nearly every day, it never gets old. In fact, I probably look like a run-of-the-mill tourist when I fly in or out of Reagan National Airport, because I still take pictures. It's as beautiful as the day I first laid eyes on it.

Over the years I've found a few favorite spots within the Capitol. The view from the Senate chaplain's office is spectacular—a panorama of the National Mall and its monuments through a window that looks like the cockpit window of the Millennium Falcon. Standing in the middle of

the eight larger-than-life paintings that encircle the Capitol rotunda is absolutely awe inspiring, and it's worth noting that the artwork depicts a
Bible study aboard the Mayflower, the baptism of Pocahontas, and perhaps the first prayer meeting in the New World.[6]

But to me the most inspiring place of its 540 rooms that span four acres
is Statuary Hall. It's a two-story semicircular room in the Old Hall, where
the House of Representatives first convened on November 17, 1800. Standing over the entrance is a marble sculpture, the *Car of History,* depicting
Clio, the muse of history, holding a book in which she chronicles events as
they occur.[7]

In 1864 Congress invited each state to nominate two prominent citizens
for permanent display in the Capitol. Thirty-eight of the now one hundred
statues stand guard in Statuary Hall. They include Philo T. Farnsworth of
Utah, the inventor of the television; Thomas Edison of Ohio, the holder of
1,093 US patents; Rosa Parks and Helen Keller of Alabama, who broke
racial and disability barriers; Jacques Marquette of Wisconsin, the Jesuit
missionary who mapped the Mississippi River; and Sacagawea of North
Dakota, the Shoshone heroine who helped Lewis and Clark explore the
Louisiana Purchase.

Walking into Statuary Hall is like walking into the Who's Who of
American history, surrounded by a great cloud of witnesses. But let me tell
you about my favorite place within my favorite room: the whispering spot.

Whispering Waves

When I first toured the Capitol more than two decades ago, our guide
revealed a secret that wasn't really a secret: the whispering spot. He stood on
one side of Statuary Hall while our tour group stood on the other side. Then
he spoke in a whisper, and sure enough, we could mysteriously and
miraculously hear the echo of his voice all the way across the room as if he
were mere inches away.

A few tall tales have been told over the years, such as the story of John
Quincy Adams pretending to be asleep at his desk while eavesdropping on

political opponents. Those stories can't be corroborated, but the physics can. The circular walls and domed ceiling of Statuary Hall allow whispering waves to travel the circumference of the room in unusual ways.

I don't know if Dr. William Thornton intended that acoustical effect, and because of the altered configuration of the room, the echoes actually occur in different places now than they did when it was the House Chamber. But the reality is this: if you stand in the right spot, you can hear a quiet whisper all the way across the room, even if it's noisy. And that's true even in the month of May, when it seems every eighth grader in America visits the nation's capital on a class trip.

When I look through the Bible, I see whispering spots everywhere.

For Abraham, it was the oak of Mamre.[8]

For Isaac, it was the well outside Nahor.[9]

For Jacob, it was Bethel.[10]

For Moses, it was a burning bush.[11]

For Joshua, it was Gilgal.[12]

For Gideon, it was the oak tree in Ophrah.[13]

For Samuel, it was the tabernacle at Shiloh.[14]

For David, it was the cave of Adullam.[15]

For Elijah, it was Mount Carmel.[16]

For Mordecai, it was the king's gate at the citadel of Susa.[17]

For Ezekiel, it was the Kebar River.[18]

For Daniel, it was an upstairs window facing Jerusalem.[19]

For Jonah, it was the belly of a whale.[20]

Let me be clear about one thing before we go any further: God can show up anywhere, anytime, anyhow. In fact, that may be why God appeared to Moses the way He did. If I had written the script, I probably would have used the pyramids as a prop, but God chose a burning bush on the back side of the desert. Why? According to rabbinic teaching, it was to show that no place is devoid of God's presence.

Yes, God's presence was uniquely manifested between the cherubim's wings above the ark of the covenant in the Holy of Holies on the Day of Atonement. But if you think God is confined to a chronological day or a geographical location, you've put God in a box—even if that box is the ark of the covenant. Don't use the Bible to box God in.

I know there are those who believe that God speaks *only* through Scripture. It's a well-meaning mistake that's often perpetrated by those who hold a high view of Scripture, as I do. I certainly believe that the Bible is in a category by itself as the inspired Word of God and that the canon is closed. But we actually undermine Scripture's authority when we discredit God's ability to speak to us now in the same ways He did in the pages of the Bible.

When I survey Scripture, I see God showing up in strange places, at strange times, in strange ways. And I don't think anything has changed. God certainly won't contradict Himself, but He is still predictably unpredictable!

He still turns appointments into divine appointments. He still uploads desires, opens doors, and inspires dreams. He still speaks through promptings and people and pain. And just as he did for Moses, He can turn any patch of ground into holy ground.

Kneeholes

In 1940 Dr. J. Edwin Orr took a group of Wheaton College students to study abroad in England. One of their stops included the Epworth Rectory. The rectory now serves as a Methodist museum, but it was the home of John Wesley, the founder of the Methodist movement.

In one of the bedrooms, there are two impressions where it is believed that John Wesley regularly knelt in prayer. As the students were getting back on the bus, Dr. Orr noticed that one student was missing. Going back upstairs, Dr. Orr found a young Billy Graham kneeling in those kneeholes and praying, "O Lord, do it again!"[21]

I live by a simple maxim: if we do what they did in the Bible, God will do what He did. He still speaks. He still heals. He still delivers. He still whispers. And there is nothing God wants to do more than to "do it again." And again, and again, and again. Of course, we must posture ourselves the way John Wesley did, the way Billy Graham did.

We'll talk about the language of desires soon enough, and I don't want us to get ahead of ourselves. But do you remember how John Wesley came to faith in Christ? He claimed that his heart was "strangely warmed" at a place called Aldersgate.[22] That sounds awfully subjective, doesn't it? But that divinely inspired feeling is a testament to the God who speaks to us at the level of emotion, and there is biblical precedent for it.

Remember the disciples who were walking from Jerusalem to Emmaus after Jesus's crucifixion and resurrection? Jesus was walking with them, was talking with them. Yet they didn't recognize Him. That might be difficult to imagine, but they didn't have a category for resurrection. Plus, their faces were "downcast."[23] When we're in an emotional funk, we often miss what is right in front of our faces. It wasn't until Jesus did what they had seen Him do before—take bread, give thanks, and break it—that His identity was revealed to them.

Do you remember what they said to each other after the fact?

Were not our hearts burning within us while he talked with us on the road and opened the Scriptures to us?[24]

Just because something isn't in the Bible doesn't make it unbiblical. By unbiblical, I mean contrary to the teachings of Scripture. There is another category—abiblical—and this carries a very different connotation. It simply means that there is no precedent in Scripture.

Does that make it unbiblical? Not necessarily. There is no precedent for pulpits or hymnals or devotionals. But as long as the methodology doesn't contradict orthodox theology, we're on good ground. We might even be on holy ground.

We shouldn't make decisions based solely on emotion, but we shouldn't ignore emotion either. In fact, one of the best ways to gauge the will of God is to discern whether or not the peace of Christ is ruling in your heart.[25] And that requires emotional intelligence. God even speaks through emotions that we can't put into words, such as the peace that passes understanding and joy unspeakable.[26]

A Pierced Ear

"Whoever has ears, let them hear."[27] Six times in the Gospels and eight times in the book of Revelation, Jesus repeats these six words. It's the simplest of statements, but the implications are exponential. The exhortation is urgent, and I believe your destiny depends on it.

When Jesus declared, "Whoever has ears, let them hear," the Jewish ear would have heard hints of Psalm 40:6: "My ears you have opened." The Hebrew word for "opened" is archaeological, meaning "to excavate" or "dig through dense material." I believe the way we do that is by listening with our inner ears. But the word for "opened" can also be translated "to pierce," which has led many Bible scholars to believe that David was tipping his hat to an ancient ritual outlined at Mount Sinai.

After serving a six-year term, a Hebrew servant was set free in the seventh year.[28] However, if a servant loved his master so much that he did not want to opt out of his servanthood, he was given the option of pledging allegiance to his master for a lifetime. How? By a sacred ritual that involved a pierced ear: "He shall take him to the door or the doorpost and pierce his ear with an awl. Then he will be his servant for life."[29]

Has your spiritual ear been pierced?

Is your inner ear consecrated to Christ?

Is the still small voice the loudest voice in your life?

The Latin word for *obey* is *obedire,* which means to "give ear."[30] Obedience starts with a pierced ear. It's tuning in to God's frequency and turning up the volume. It's obeying His whispers, even if a thousand people are screaming something different.

"Tell me to what you pay attention," said the Spanish philosopher José Ortega y Gasset, "and I will tell you who are you."[31] You will eventually be shaped in the image of the loudest voice in your life—the voice you listen to most.

Genuine listening is ultimately an act of submission. If you're married and you've had a "lively discussion" with your spouse, you know of what I speak. The natural reaction is to raise your voice, isn't it? But that rarely solves the problem. Actually, it never does. The solution is shutting your mouth and opening your ears. The way we submit to one another is by genuinely, thoughtfully, patiently, and carefully listening. And a relationship with God is no different.

The Inner Ear

It's hard for us to imagine that the solution to our problems is listening, but listening is the litmus test. To fully appreciate its importance, a little ear anatomy is necessary.

Sound waves crash into our ears like ocean waves on a beach. They travel through a labyrinth that author Diane Ackerman likens to a "maniacal miniature golf course" complete with "curlicues, branches, roundabouts, relays, levers, hydraulics, and feedback loops."[32]

The outer ear functions like a funnel, catching the sound. After traveling through the ear canal and hitting the eardrum, the vibrations bump into three of the tiniest bones in the body: the hammer, anvil, and stirrup. From the middle ear, the vibrations spiral through a snail-shaped tube called the cochlea, which contains thousands of microscopic hair cells that amplify the sound along its way. From there the eighth cranial nerve transmits impulses like Morse code to the auditory cortex, where pitch, volume, tone, distance, direction, and meaning are translated into actionable information.

Again, don't tell me you've never experienced a miracle. You experience one every time sound makes its mysterious journey through your outer, middle, and inner ear.

One of the mysterious capabilities of the human ear is tuning out certain sounds while tuning in others. When I played basketball in college, no matter how many people were yelling and screaming, I could discern my dad's voice above the crowd. This capability "is possible," notes Ackerman, "because we actually hear things twice."[33]

Audiologically, there is a short time delay between sound waves hitting the outer ear and reaching the inner ear. So some things we listen to once, others twice. When Jesus said, "Whoever has ears, let them hear," I think it's an exhortation to listen not once but twice. It's in that gap between the first hearing and second hearing where we discern the promptings of the Holy Spirit.

Don't just listen to God with the outer ear. That's how things go in one ear and out the other. Give God a second hearing, with the inner ear. That's how truth gets from your head to your heart of hearts. And maybe, just maybe, that's how to get from the outer courts into the inner courts—the Holy Place, where God manifests His presence!

Inverse-Square Law

The whispering spot in the United States Capitol may be the most famous whispering gallery, but it's not the only one. The whisper effect was first discovered in 1878 at Saint Paul's Cathedral in London by Lord Rayleigh. Rayleigh won the 1904 Nobel Prize for his discovery of the element argon, atomic number 18. But his true passion, his lifelong fascination, was sound. In fact, Lord Rayleigh has a low-frequency sound wave named after him. The Rayleigh wave is inaudible to the human ear, but it's the frequency that birds, insects, and other animals use to communicate infrasonically.

Lord Rayleigh, a devout Anglican, explained the mystery of traveling whispers in Saint Paul's Cathedral through brilliantly designed sound experiments showing that one whisper produced four, five, even six echoes. According to the inverse-square law, sound should decay in intensity as an inverse of distance.[34] As sound travels, it disperses, so hypothetically our words should have half the energy at twice the distance. Whispering spots are a unique exception to this rule. Whispers in Saint Paul's can be heard loud and clear long distances away because of the curvature of the ceilings and walls.

You can guess where this is going, can't you?

Just as there are whispering spots in the physical realm, there are whispering spots in the spiritual realm. And I want to help you discover your whispering spot—the place you go to hear God's whisper, the place where His voice echoes loudest and longest, the place where He speaks via healing and revealing, convicting and creating.

God's voice is not subject to the inverse-square law or any other law of nature for that matter. His voice does not diminish over space and time. The God who defined the laws of physics in the first place has the power to defy said laws. The God who created the sun can make the sun stand still. The great irony, of course, is that when He breaks the laws of physics, we call it a miracle. And it is. But it's really the second miracle in a sequence. Making the sun stand still is miraculous, but so is keeping Earth in orbit. Celebrate the second miracle, but don't discount the first one. It's a double miracle.

All of that is to say this: the sound of God's voice does not decay with distance.

The prophet Isaiah said it this way:

So is my word that goes out from my mouth:
    It will not return to me empty,
but will accomplish what I desire
    and achieve the purpose for which I sent it.[35]

Remember, God's first four words are still echoing at the outer edges of the universe, creating galaxies everywhere they go! What's true of those first four words is true of every whisper. As I inventory my life, I realize that all the blessings, all the breakthroughs, are really echoes of God's whispers. I've also learned there are certain places and postures that help me hear the voice of God more clearly.

The Tent of Meeting

When I was in college, one verse affected me more than any other. It might seem a little strange at first, but it inspired my first whispering spot. It's the story about the tent of meeting that Moses pitched outside the camp of

Israel while the Israelites wandered the wilderness. My take on it is that Moses pitched it outside the camp so he'd be out of earshot. He was tired of the Israelites' incessant grumbling, complaining, and murmuring, and he desperately needed a quiet place—a whispering spot.

Moses is the lead actor in this story, but there is an extra scene at the very end.

> Then Moses would return to the camp, but his young aide Joshua son of Nun did not leave the tent.[36]

Have you ever wondered why God chose Joshua to succeed Moses? For starters, he was one of the two spies who brought back a positive report when the Israelites first explored Canaan.[37] The other ten spies, who had very loud voices, brought back negative reports. The people listened to the wrong voices, and it cost them forty years!

But there is a second reason God chose Joshua to succeed Moses. God trusts most those who know Him best, and those who know Him best are those who have spent the most time with Him. Since Joshua never left the tent of meeting, he was the obvious choice.

When I was in college, I wanted to be Joshua. Every time there was an altar call, I responded. Why? Because I didn't want to leave whatever gift God wanted to give me at the altar. That's an opportunity cost I didn't want to pay. I also created a "tent of meeting" that turned into my first whispering spot.

Nearly every day after lunch I would sneak into the chapel. The lights were off, and the chapel was empty except for an occasional janitor sighting. I'd climb the stairs to the balcony, where I'd pace and pray. We didn't have Fitbits back then, but I bet I walked a hundred miles as I prayed my senior year. That's where I learned to discern the voice of God, including a check in my spirit that kept me out of what could have been a bad situation (which I'll detail when I talk about the language of doors).

In seminary my whispering spot was the four-hundred-square-foot apartment my wife and I rented on the campus of Trinity International

University in Deerfield, Illinois. Lora worked while I took classes, so I had the apartment to myself most days. It was there that God picked me up and dusted me off after our failed church plant.

One of my longest-standing whispering spots was a marble pillar in front of Union Station in Washington, DC, where National Community Church met for thirteen years. I would perch myself on that pillar on Saturday nights, talking and listening to God.

My current whispering spot, and my all-time favorite, is the rooftop of Ebenezers Coffeehouse. I get great reception up there! When you pray on top of a miracle that God has already done, it's hard not to have faith. That coffeehouse was once a whisper, and God continues to whisper to me there.

When I first started praying in the chapel balcony or on the rooftop of Ebenezers, they were just "spots." Over time they turned into whispering spots. Whispering spots don't have to be exotic. Quite the contrary. They're often as ordinary as a closet that turns into a prayer closet. The key isn't geography; it's consistency.

If you show up, God will too!

Listening Point

In 1956 environmentalist Sigurd Olson built a small cabin on the banks of Burntside Lake in northern Minnesota. The naming of lake homes is customary, especially in the land of ten thousand lakes. Most names are rather predictable, but Olson was a little more intentional. His objective in building the cabin was to "hear all that was worth listening for,"[38] so he named it Listening Point.

Listening doesn't happen by default; it happens by design. You have to go outside the camp and build a tent of meeting. You have to seek solitude, seek silence. You have to ruthlessly eliminate distractions. And you have to turn some voices down or tune them out altogether. It might be as innocent as talk radio or as innocuous as social media. Why not turn off the radio and talk to God during your commute? Or fast from social media for a season? Or take a silent retreat?

I don't want to overspiritualize the importance of a whispering spot, but I don't want to underspiritualize it either. Even if you take spirituality out of the equation, you need a space or place to get some peace and quiet. If you live in a city, as I do, it's not easy. And if you're a parent of little children, it might be ten minutes during nap time. No matter, you have to be bound and determined to find a time and a place.

Susanna Wesley raised seventeen children in a very small home, so solitude was hard to come by. Her whispering spot was a rocking chair in the middle of the room. When she threw a blanket over herself, it turned into her tent of meeting.[39]

Perhaps that's what inspired her son John to kneel next to his bed.

Thomas Edison had a "thinking chair."[40]

Alexander Graham Bell had a "dreaming place" overlooking the Grand River.[41]

Henry David Thoreau skipped stones on Walden Pond.

Then there was Ludwig van Beethoven, who began his day at dawn with a cup of coffee that he prepared with great care by counting sixty beans per cup.[42] He sat at his desk until early afternoon and then took a stroll to reinvigorate his mind. He carried a pencil and a few sheets of music paper in his pocket to record chance musical thoughts.[43]

Your whispering spot will be as unique as you are, but you need to find a time, find a place.

May I ask a seemingly silly question? Have you ever tried setting up a meeting with someone without designating a time and place? Imagine asking someone when he wants to meet, and he says, "Whenever." Or asking him where he wants to meet, and he says, "Wherever." Good luck with that meeting! I appreciate flexibility, but that meeting is never going to happen except by accident.

A Defining Decision

Solitude is one key to hearing the voice of God, no question, but it needs a counterbalance. Hearing the voice of God is not a solo sport; it's a team sport. And one of the best ways to hear His voice is to get around those people who do. Is there someone in your life who seems to hear God more frequently, more clearly, than you do? Get as close to that person as you can. You just might hear, or overhear, the voice of God!

Dick Eastman is one of those people for me. I'll never forget the day he and I sat in my office and he shared about a defining moment in his life.[44] Someone had given him a cassette-tape recording of "The Holy Hour!" by Archbishop Fulton J. Sheen speaking to a group of nuns. The recording quality was so poor that Dick could barely hear what was on it, but he heard the voice of God loud and clear. That cassette tape changed the course of his life because of a defining decision he made after listening to it.

The eighty-year-old archbishop revealed to the nuns the secret of his success as perhaps the most influential Catholic in America at the time other than the pope. It could come across as a little condescending out of context, but the older you get, the more blunt you can be. There's no time to dillydally. Sheen said, "You nuns are far more intelligent than me. So why am I speaking to you? . . . I'll tell you why." Then the archbishop answered his own question: "Because my words have power." And why did he believe his words had power? "My words have power because for fifty-five years, 365 days a year, I've spent an hour in God's presence."

As Dick listened to that crackly cassette tape, he came under intense conviction. When he shared this story with me, it was more than forty years after the fact, yet there were tears in his eyes. He said, "Mark, I couldn't say that for seven days!" Something snapped in Dick's spirit that day. He made a defining decision to spend an hour a day, every day, in the presence of God. Dick has now practiced this daily ritual for nearly as long as the archbishop had.

For most of his ministry, Dick Eastman has served as international president of Every Home for Christ, an organization that has led an estimated 191,000,000 people to a faith decision and started more than 324,000 church fellowships called Christ Groups. Is it any wonder why? Is it any secret how? And God wants to do it again through you.

Finding a whispering spot takes time and patience.

Finding a whispering spot takes effort and intentionality.

That said, we aren't always the ones who decide when or where or how it happens. Sometimes we find whispering spots, but sometimes whispering spots find us.

Sometimes this happens because of a crisis that drives us to our knees, such as Paul and Silas getting thrown into prison.[45] In my experience tough spots often turn into whispering spots. I've heard God in some pretty exotic places, including the Grand Canyon and the Andes Mountains, but not as clearly as I heard Him after regaining consciousness in the intensive-care unit at Washington Hospital Center after two days on a respirator. That hospital room was a whispering spot in the wee hours of the morning.

Sometimes it's a celebration, like King David dancing before the Lord when he brought the ark back to Jerusalem.[46] When was the last time you lost all inhibition and worshipped God with all your might, as David did?

A Defining Moment

A few years after making the decision to give God an hour a day, Dick Eastman felt led to spend an entire day doing nothing but worshipping Him. He wasn't entirely sure how to do it, but he decided to give it a go during a trip to Washington, DC, because he had a day with no commitments on his calendar.

Dick started worshipping God in his hotel room right when he woke up. He continued worshipping while he checked out and ate breakfast. Then he decided to find a park outside the Beltway where he could take a long walk through the woods and worship without distraction. Dick eventually came to a clearing in a grove of trees, and he felt as if he wanted to worship God in a way that he never had before. He had read about David dancing before the Lord, but he admitted, "Mark, I grew up in a church where you don't dance! I didn't know how to dance, I didn't know what to do, but I just felt like I should try."

After double-checking to make sure no one was watching, Dick started dancing in the middle of that clearing. His dancing was so bad that Dick actually started laughing out loud at himself. When he was done, he wondered how that could possibly have been pleasing to the Lord. Dick very meekly said, "Lord, was that okay?" The Lord whispered back, *You have no idea how much joy you just brought Me!*

I live by an Oswald Chambers's maxim: "Let God be as original with other people as He is with you."[47] So I'm not suggesting that you find the nearest clearing in a grove of trees and dance before the Lord. In fact, our family was out at a restaurant the night I had shared that story in a sermon, and for whatever reason I busted out a dance move. My youngest son, Josiah, was spot on: "Dad, this isn't a clearing in a grove of trees!"

Don't just go out and do what Dick Eastman or your spiritual hero did. That's a spiritual cop-out. Copycat spirituality is short lived. Learn to listen to God's voice, and then do what He says. That might mean doing something different. Or it might mean doing exactly what you're doing but with a different attitude. Either way, quit putting God in your box.

I have a little formula that I've shared in other books, so I won't completely unpack it here. But it bears repeating: change of pace + change of place = change of perspective. Sometimes a little change of scenery goes a long way in helping us hear God in new ways. So does doing something you've never done before.

If you want God to do something new, you can't keep doing the same old thing. You have to dare to be different, and that includes listening in a new way. That's what learning these seven love languages of God is all about.

Let the games begin!

Part Two

THE SEVEN LOVE LANGUAGES

4

SIGN LANGUAGE

*God spoke to our ancestors . . . at many
times and in various ways.*

—HEBREWS 1:1

On August 10, 1874, twenty-seven-year-old Alexander Graham Bell sat
on a blanket near a bluff overlooking the Grand River in Ontario,
Canada. He called it his dreaming place. He had spent the morning tinker-
ing with a phonautograph, an apparatus that mimicked the action of the
human ear. His passion was deaf education, but in a stroke of genius, he
began to wonder whether electric currents could be made to simulate sound
waves and transmit voices electrically.[1]

"The day is coming," wrote Bell in a letter to his father, "when telegraph
wires will be laid on to houses just like water or gas—and friends converse
with each without leaving home."[2]

It was a bold vision for a brave new world.

On the evening of March 10, 1876, Bell and his assistant, Thomas
Watson, were up late trying to perfect the clarity of their sound transmission.
That's when Watson heard these immortal words: "Mr. Watson, come
here—I want to see you." The irony was the urgency with which Bell spoke
them. He had just spilled battery acid on himself, so this could be considered the first 911 call too![3]

Later that same year the city of Philadelphia hosted the World's Fair.

Among the 22,742 exhibits were sewing machines, canned foods, bananas, and root beer. The exhibition opened with a speech by President Ulysses S. Grant, who had invited a distinguished guest, Pedro II, emperor of Brazil. Two weeks earlier the emperor *just happened* to visit Boston, where he *just happened* to meet Alexander Graham Bell. That one meeting would prove to be quite providential.

On June 25 of that year, the Committee of Electrical Awards was scheduled to judge the World's Fair entrants in this category. The guest judge? None other than Pedro II. The blazing sun almost cut the contest short, but that's when the emperor spotted Bell. The entourage of judges, some of whom had stripped down to their undershirts, wanted to call it quits, but Pedro insisted that they examine Bell's exhibit. He put the telephone receiver to his ear while Bell spoke into the mouthpiece some distance away, and the look on the emperor's face was nothing short of pure astonishment as he exclaimed, "This thing speaks!"[4]

Dr. Joseph Henry, the first secretary of the Smithsonian Institute and one of the judges that day, called it "the greatest marvel hitherto achieved by the telegraph."[5] The *New York Herald* called it "almost supernatural."[6]

Needless to say, Bell won the gold medal for electrical equipment. And the rest is history, thanks to Pedro II, emperor of Brazil.

Various Ways

If there is such a thing as a biblical understatement, "God spoke to our ancestors . . . at many times and in various ways"[7] qualifies. God's ability to speak in strange and mysterious ways is nothing short of astounding. He spoke to Moses via the burning bush. He spoke to Pharaoh through ten signs and wonders. He spoke to Hezekiah via illness. He spoke to Babylonian astrologers with the stars. He spoke to Belshazzar via a disembodied hand that inscribed "MENE, MENE, TEKEL, PARSIN"[8] on the palace wall. And my personal favorite, He spoke to Balaam through a donkey!

I bet the look on Balaam's face was a little like Emperor Pedro's expression. And I wouldn't be surprised if Balaam said the same thing:

"This thing speaks!" The implication? If God can speak through Balaam's donkey,[9] he can speak through anything!

Let me be absolutely clear about one thing. After highlighting the various ways in which God speaks, the writer of Hebrews zeroes in on God's greatest revelation: Jesus Christ. He is the full and final revelation of God. He is the Son of Man and the Son of God. He is the Creator of all things and the Heir of all things. He is "the way and the truth and the life."[10] And at His name, every knee will bow and every tongue will confess.[11]

Does God still speak in "various ways"? I believe He does. I believe God speaks in the same ways now as He did then, but now we have the distinct advantage of having Scripture as our sounding board.

To believe that God speaks *only* through the Bible is to handcuff the God of the Bible as the Bible has revealed Him to us. Yes, Scripture provides our checks and balances. And God will never say anything that is contrary to His good, pleasing, and perfect will as revealed in Scripture. But God still speaks in various ways, and we'll explore seven of those languages in the pages that follow.

Eight Kinds of Smart

More than three decades ago, a Harvard professor named Dr. Howard Gardner wrote a groundbreaking book called *Frames of Mind*. Dr. Gardner popularized the theory of multiple intelligences. Simply put, different people are smart in different ways. His original categories had eight types of intelligence: word smart, number smart, picture smart, body smart, music smart, people smart, self smart, and nature smart.[12]

Let me give you just a couple of examples.

When Wolfgang Amadeus Mozart was a boy, he visited the Sistine Chapel in Rome, where he was enchanted by a piece of music by Gregorio Allegri. Mozart asked for a copy of the music, but the Sistine Chapel had decreed that *Miserere* could be performed only inside the Sistine Chapel and couldn't be copied under any circumstances. Mozart attended one more performance and then used his phonographic memory to write out the entire musical score from memory! I have no idea if Mozart was body smart or number smart, but he was definitely music smart.[13]

A hundred years before the invention of calculators, Johann Martin Zacharias Dase calculated pi correctly to two hundred places in less than two months. He could multiply two eight-digit numbers in fifty-four seconds, two forty-digit numbers in forty minutes, and two hundred-digit numbers in eight and three-fourths hours. Dase could perform calculations for weeks on end. He'd stop calculating at bedtime, store everything in memory, and pick up the next morning right where he left off. He could even count the number of sheep in a flock after a single glance! I have no idea if Dase was music smart or people smart, but it's safe to say he was number smart.[14]

As a child, Bart Conner displayed an unusual talent: he could walk on his hands almost as well as his feet. He performed his signature move at parties quite frequently. He even figured out how to go up and down stairs on his hands! Walking on your hands isn't exactly a marketable skill, unless, of course, you're a gymnast. I have no idea if America's most decorated male gymnast is picture smart or nature smart, but he's definitely body smart.[15]

We are smart in different ways, and that's a testament to the God who created us. We also relate to God in different ways, and that's a testament to a God who is big enough to be heard by anyone and everyone, anywhere and everywhere. We'll explore the way spirituality filters through personality when we get to the language of desires, but thinkers and feelers relate to God differently. So do introverts and extroverts. And that goes for all sixteen personality types in the Myers-Briggs matrix, all nine Enneagram types, and all four DISC profiles.

What does that have to do with hearing the voice of God? First, we all hear Him a little differently.

This is cause for humility, first and foremost. Can we admit a measure of subjectivity based on personality and prejudice? And while we're at it, can we admit faulty assumptions and false motives? We usually hear what we *want* to hear and turn a deaf ear to everything else. But remember the package deal? If we don't listen to *everything* God has to say, we eventually won't hear *anything* He has to say. And we probably need to hear *most* what we want to hear *least*. But this I know for sure: His tone of voice is always loving. Sometimes it's tough love in the form of rebuke or discipline, but it's loving, nonetheless. In fact, it's loving all the more![16]

Second, God speaks in different languages.

God speaks to different personalities in different ways. The way Jesus related to His disciples was as different as Peter, James, and John. God is big enough to speak as many languages as there are people. In this section we'll focus on seven love languages. We'll start with Scripture, the first and final Word. Then we'll explore six secondary languages: desires, doors, dreams, people, promptings, and pain.

Silent Messages

At nineteen months of age, Helen Keller lost her vision and hearing after a bout with meningitis. And because she couldn't hear, she also lost her ability to speak. That left her blind, deaf, and mute. Of the three, Keller considered deafness her greatest incapacity. "The problems of deafness are deeper and more complex," said Keller. "For it means the loss of the most vital stimulus— the sound of the voice that brings language, sets thoughts astir and keeps us in the intellectual company of man."[17]

Helen Keller famously said, "The only thing worse than blindness is having sight but no vision." Perhaps the same could be said of those who have hearing but don't really listen.

Helen Keller could have given up on life, totally isolated from the outside world. Instead, she learned to listen in a different way. She learned to "listen" to music by literally laying hands on the radio. Her sense of touch became so finely tuned that she could hear the difference between horns and strings with her fingertips.[18] She also learned to listen by feeling a person's lips, face, and larynx, including the lips of the second-greatest influence in her life after Anne Sullivan: Alexander Graham Bell.

We don't just listen with our ears.

We listen with our eyes, with our hearts.

That's how we discern promptings, people, and pain.

We don't just read Scripture.

We read desires and doors and dreams.

Here's a helpful way of thinking about these six secondary languages.

In 1971 psychologist Albert Mehrabian published *Silent Messages,* which included his pioneering research on nonverbal communication. When it comes to credibility, Mehrabian found that we assign 55 percent of the weight to body language, 38 percent to tone, and 7 percent to actual words.[19]

Scripture is made up of actual words, and it certainly represents far more than 7 percent of God's revelation. It "is useful for teaching, rebuking, correcting and training in righteousness."[20] But God also speaks via body language: His body, the church. I call it the language of people. And God speaks through different tones of voice, including the language of desires and the language of pain. But when it comes to interpreting body language and tone, we desperately need the gift of discernment.

It takes discernment to spot closed doors and open doors.

It takes discernment to recognize God-given dreams.

It takes discernment to know which desires are from God.

It takes discernment to obey the promptings of God.

It takes discernment to put pain into perspective.

It takes discernment to read people.

The person without the Spirit does not accept the things that come from the Spirit of God but considers them foolishness, and cannot understand them because they are discerned only through the Spirit.[21]

The English word *discern* comes from the Greek word *epignosis,* which means "knowledge gained by firsthand contact." It's experiential. In other words, it's not book smarts as much as it's street smarts. And it's fine-tuned over time. But do you know the quickest way to learn a new language? It's not sitting in a classroom or reading a book; it's full immersion. You have to put yourself in the position where that's all you can hear, all you can speak.

The same is true of these seven languages. You have to jump into the deep end and start swimming.

Cross-Check

Our Capitol Hill campus is located just a few blocks from Gallaudet University, the first school in the world for the advanced education of the deaf. With our close proximity, we've had many members of the deaf community attend NCC since day one. And I've come to appreciate our interpreters, who preach my message using manual communication while I use verbal communication.

Can God speak audibly? Absolutely! But more often than not, He speaks in "sign language." I know this makes those who try to live by "the letter of the law" a little uncomfortable, and I understand why. Signs can be subjective. We'd rather rely on *sola Scriptura*. The problem with that limitation is that God speaks via sign language in Scripture. That's our precedent. And it's part and parcel of living a Spirit-led life.

If we ignore the signs God sends our way, we miss the miracle. Or worse—like Pilate, who ignored the sign God gave his wife in a dream[22]—we become unwitting accomplices to the Enemy's schemes.

God's ability to speak in signs is limitless. It can be as obvious as a burning bush, as strange as Balaam's donkey, or as subtle as a whisper. But generally God speaks through divine appointments and divine timing. I call them supernatural synchronicities. And although it's not easy to discern coincidence from providence, I make no apologies for believing that God is in the business of strategically positioning us in the right place at the right time with the right people. I stand by, stand on, His providential promises.

God is preparing good works in advance.[23]

God is ordering our footsteps.[24]

God is working all things together for good for those who love Him.[25]

Signs are as easy to misinterpret as they are to interpret, so here's an important rule of thumb: cross-check your interpretation against Scripture. I know lots of people who have excused sinful behavior as God's sovereignty because they confused temptation with opportunity. Just because sin knocks on the front door doesn't mean God is giving you a green light. It's not an "opportunity" if you have to compromise your integrity.

If Jacob's son Joseph had used that faulty logic, he would have slept with Potiphar's wife.[26] Sure, he would have avoided his prison sentence that was based on false accusations, but two nations would have been wiped off the face of the earth by famine because Joseph would have missed his divine appointment with a fellow prisoner that led to his divine appointment with Pharaoh. My point? The sovereignty of God is way past our pay grade. Instead of spending all our energy trying to figure out the future, we need to focus on doing the right thing, right here, right now.

God will never lead us to do something that is contrary to His good, pleasing, and perfect will as revealed in Scripture. That said, Scripture doesn't reveal the logistics. That's the job of the Holy Spirit. Scripture doesn't reveal whether we should go *here or there*. It doesn't nuance whether we should do *this, that, or the other thing*. And although its truth is timeless, it doesn't reveal *now or later*. Scripture gives us guidelines, but the Holy Spirit is our Guide.

A New Language

Remember Dr. Alfred Tomatis, the otolaryngologist who treated the opera singer who couldn't hit the note he couldn't hear? He encountered a very similar case involving Venetian opera singers who were unable to pronounce the letter *r* with the tips of their tongues.[27] I appreciate that problem because even after four years of studying Spanish, I was unable to roll my *r*'s. That makes the Spanish word *perro* sound pretty pedestrian!

The problem was particularly troublesome for these Venetian opera singers because Italian librettos are full of the *r* phoneme. Instead of saying the *r* sound, they substituted *l*, which sounds about as silly as my Spanglish. Why couldn't they sing the *r* sound? Because it wasn't part of their Venetian dialect. They couldn't sing it because they weren't used to hearing it.

To remedy the situation, Dr. Tomatis did what any good teacher would do: he employed good old-fashioned repetition. With practice and patience, those opera singers learned to hear the *r*. And once they heard it, they could sing it.

Linguists in the tradition of philosopher Noam Chomsky view language as not just an ancient instinct but a "special gift."[28] And I agree. Dogs bark, cows moo, and mockingbirds sing. But our ability to acquire language by speaking and listening is unique among God's creation. As such, I believe it's one dimension of the image of God. So to grow in the likeness of God is to steward language better, both in terms of speaking and listening. But listening comes first. And it might be twice as important, given that God has given each of us two ears and one larynx.

These seven love languages are spiritual languages, but they are *languages*. What makes us think that they are any easier, any faster, to acquire than English or Arabic? Rome wasn't built in a day, and Italian isn't learned overnight.

Babies have to hear their parents repeat sounds thousands of times before they are able to enunciate those same sounds. It takes them between nine and twelve months to voice the first intelligible word. On average, babies have only five words in their vocabulary on their first birthday.[29] But that's when the language explosion begins. By the age of six, the average child has accumulated fourteen thousand words![30]

Learning a new language can be a little frustrating at first, and it requires a willingness to sound a little foolish too. But if you keep listening, the language explosion will eventually happen.

I can't promise the process will be easy, but I hope you enjoy the journey. The key to learning is the love of learning. And the same is true of hearing the voice of God. It starts with longing to hear, loving to listen.

At some point most people settle for secondhand spirituality. But listening to those who listen to God is no substitute for seeking Him yourself. If you become reliant upon others for inspiration, that's called spiritual codependency.

God wants to speak to *you*.

Yes, you!

One last exhortation.

Depending on your spiritual background, some of these seven languages will seem like foreign languages. That means they might take a little longer to learn. But that is often where the greatest discoveries are made.

I grew up in a church that didn't recognize Lent. In fact, I managed to get into my second year of seminary without having any idea what Ash Wednesday was. And I didn't discover it in a class; I discovered it as part of the studio audience at *The Oprah Winfrey Show*! The producer came out to brief the audience before the show began, and I turned to Lora and whispered, "He's got dirt on his forehead." I had a hard time not laughing out loud because I could hardly conceive of a television producer not noticing dirt on his forehead. To quote the rock band Queen, "You got mud on yo' face, you big disgrace."[31] Well, the joke was on the seminary student who didn't know it was Ash Wednesday.

I was in my thirties before I started observing Lent in a meaningful way. Over the years it has become a catalyst in my annual spiritual rhythm, but it wasn't part of my dialect growing up. I had to acquire the vocabulary, and it's become an acquired taste.

This is my prayer for you. In the pages that follow, may you learn to discern the voice of God in new ways.

God speaks through His Word. That's our starting point. He whispers to us through doors, dreams, and desires. He converses with us through promptings, pain, and other people. Some of these languages will be more natural for you than others, but I'd wager there are ways to grow your vocabulary and become more fluent in all seven languages.

5

THE KEY OF KEYS

The First Language: Scripture

All Scripture is God-breathed.

—2 Timothy 3:16

On April 14, 1755, General Edward Braddock sailed up the Potomac River to Georgetown, a sleepy little town on the banks of the river. The British army anchored long enough to pick up a new recruit, a twenty-three-year-old Virginia planter named George Washington. Washington served as Braddock's aide-de-camp during the ill-fated Battle of the Monongahela, and it's a miracle he survived. Two horses were shot out from under him, and four musket balls passed through his coat. Washington didn't just hear musket balls whistling past his ears; he heard the still small voice whispering. "Death was leveling my Companions on every side of me," wrote Washington in a letter to his brother. "But, by the All-powerful Dispensations of Providence, I have been protected."[1]

Now let's go back to the place where Braddock anchored his ship. In the city named after Washington, just past the place where Constitution Avenue turns into the Theodore Roosevelt Bridge, there is a nondescript stone well with a small historical marker beside it. There is a manhole cover on top of it and a ladder inside of it. Sixteen feet below the surface is a rock: Braddock's Rock. It marks the place where General Braddock first landed, and it's the oldest landmark in the nation's capital.

According to legend some of that rock was used as foundation stone for the White House and Capitol. But the true significance of that stone is that it served as the starting point for the earliest surveys of Washington, DC. On old maps it's inscribed as the Key of Keys. That was the name given to Braddock's Rock because it established the coordinate system for the entire city. Every principal meridian and baseline was measured from that initial point.

Whether we're aware of it or not, we all have a key of keys.

Epistemology is the branch of philosophy concerned with the nature of knowledge. It asks, "How do we know that we know?" And whether we consciously construct it or not, we all have an epistemological starting point by which we survey all of life. It establishes our moral baseline, delineating between right and wrong. For some, it fluctuates as much as the latest fad. For others, it's as fixed as the scientific method. For me, it's as tried and true as the Bible. And I make no apologies for that. The Bible is not just my starting point; it's the final authority when it comes to matters of faith and doctrine. I believe the Bible to be the inspired Word of God—Truth with a capital *T*.

The challenge is that we live in a culture where tolerance has been elevated above truth. It's considered wrong to say that something is wrong, and I think that's wrong. I certainly want to be known more for what I'm *for* than what I'm *against*. And truth shouldn't be used as a weapon. But to think that everybody is right and nobody is wrong is as silly as pretending that everybody wins and nobody loses. Come on, you know the T-ballers are keeping track of the score! And even if *not* keeping score works for one season in Little League, it doesn't work in the real world. When truth is sacrificed on the altar of tolerance, it might seem as though everybody wins, but in reality everybody loses. God calls us to a higher standard than tolerance. It's called truth, and it's always coupled with grace.[2]

Grace means *I'll love you no matter what.*

Truth means *I'll be honest with you no matter what.*

That's my principal meridian.

Now let me back up just a bit.

Prized Possession

I have a twenty-five-year addiction that started with the eight-hundred-page biography of Albert Einstein I read in college.[3] I fell in love with books, and I started reading anything and everything I could get my hands on. Part of that love of learning was Einstein's exhortation in that very book: "Never lose a holy curiosity."[4] Part of it was pure necessity.

When I started pastoring National Community Church, I lacked both ministry experience and life experience. My ministry résumé included one summer internship and one failed church plant. That's it. My life experience amounted to just twenty-five trips around the sun, and it was a rather sheltered existence at that. I needed to borrow as much experience as I could, and I did that through books.

Around that time I heard that the average author invests approximately two years of life experience into every book he or she writes, so I figured I was gaining two years of life experience with every book I read. In my twenties I averaged reading more than two hundred books a year, so I was gaining four hundred years of life experience each year! To date, I've read at least thirty-five hundred books, so I'm at least seven thousand years old in book years!

Simply put, I love books. But one book falls in a category of its own: the Bible. At least two things make the Bible absolutely unique. First, it is "living and active."[5] We don't just read the Bible; the Bible reads us. The Spirit who inspired the ancient writers as they wrote is the same Spirit who inspires modern-day readers as they read. The Holy Spirit is on both sides of the equation. The apostle Paul described Scripture as "God-breathed."[6] When we read Scripture, we're inhaling what the Holy Spirit exhaled thousands of years ago. We're hearing the whisper of God in breath tones.

Second, we never get to the bottom of the Bible. According to rabbinic tradition, every word of Scripture has seventy faces and six hundred thousand meanings.[7] In other words, it's kaleidoscopic. No matter how many times we read the Bible, it never gets old, because it's timeless and timely.

The Bible was composed by more than forty writers over fifteen centuries in three languages on three continents. Those authors range from farmers and fishermen and kings to poets, prophets, and prisoners of war. It covers nearly every subject matter under the sun: law and history, poetry and prophecy, cosmology and theology. Yet despite the fact that it touches on hundreds of controversial topics, it doesn't contradict itself.[8] In fact, it reads like one book from start to finish. And that's because there is one Author, the Spirit of God.

We take the Bible for granted, and I think that's because we can get it in dozens of different translations with any type and color of cover we want. But let's not forget that ancient scribes would devote entire lifetimes to making *one copy* of the sacred text, and translators such as John Wycliffe and William Tyndale gave their lives to provide us their translations.

My most prized earthly possession is a time-tattered Bible that belonged to my grandfather Elmer Johnson. The pages of the third improved edition of the 1934 Thompson Chain-Reference Bible are worn thin from use, so thin that my grandfather had to tape them together. I love reading the verses he underlined and the notes he scribbled in the margins. This might sound mystical, but that Bible connects me to my grandfather in a way that escapes words. And his well-used Bible is a testament to his well-lived life. It reminds me of something Charles Spurgeon said: "A Bible that's falling apart usually belongs to someone who isn't."[9]

Bibliolatry

Reading the Bible cover to cover is a spiritual best practice, and there is no better way to learn to discern God's voice. Theologian J. I. Packer went so far as to say, "Every Christian worth his salt ought to read the Bible from cover to cover every year."[10] Most of us fall short on that count, but it's hard to argue with, isn't it? However, the goal isn't getting through the Bible; the goal is getting the Bible through us.

There is a very subtle form of idolatry called bibliolatry. It involves treating the Bible as an end in itself instead of a means to an end. The goal of Bible knowledge isn't just Bible knowledge. After all, "knowledge puffs up."[11] The goal is learning to recognize and respond to your heavenly Father's voice so you can grow in intimacy with Him.

But make no mistake, the Bible can be misused and abused. You have to look no further than the devil himself, who tried to use Scripture to tempt Jesus: "If you are the Son of God, tell this stone to become bread."[12] That was a low blow, considering that Jesus had been fasting for forty days. But we do the same thing when we use truth to bully others. Yes, the Bible is our sword. It's our best offense, our best defense. But when we misinterpret the truth, we're abusing the Bible. Remember how Jesus responded? By rightly dividing the Word: "Man does not live on bread alone."[13]

We need to heed Paul's exhortation: "Study to shew thyself approved unto God, a workman that needeth not to be ashamed, rightly dividing the word of truth."[14] If we don't rightly divide the Word of God, we divide the body of Christ. And that's the opposite of holiness, which means "wholeness."

I have a little formula that I share quite frequently: the Holy Spirit + caffeine = awesome. As the pastor of a church that owns a coffeehouse, I'm not joking. And my office is right above the coffeehouse! But here's a more serious equation: Holy Scripture – Holy Spirit = bibliolatry. When we take the Holy Spirit out of the equation, we're left with the letter of the law. And the letter of the law isn't life giving. What you end up with is rule lawyering like the Pharisees and a lifeless religion called legalism.

One of the jobs of the Holy Spirit is quickening, and it's the difference between information and transformation. Ironically, *quicken* is the same word used to describe physical resurrection.[15] In much the same way, the Holy Spirit defibrillates our spirits with His Word so we experience a little resurrection every time we read God's Word.

He brings dreams back to life.

He revives faith, hope, and love.
He delivers on promises we've given up on.

The Transitive Property

On the morning of August 16, 1996, I was just three verses into the book of Joshua when God quickened a promise that jumped off the page and into my spirit.

I will give you every place where you set your foot, as I promised Moses.[16]

As I read that promise, I felt prompted to pray a perimeter all the way around Capitol Hill, the place God had called us to pastor. I immediately embarked on a 4.7-mile prayer walk, which I detail in *The Circle Maker*. When I prayed that prayer, I never thought we'd own a single piece of property, and that wasn't the original intent. But God has reasons that are often beyond human reason. Two decades later we own half a dozen properties, valued at more than $50 million, on that prayer circle. Coincidence? I think not.

One of those miracle properties is a 125-year-old castle that sits on a city block we purchased for $29 million. First of all, I did not have a category for that kind of price tag twenty years ago. I still don't. But it's no coincidence that we signed the contract on the castle eighteen years *to the day* after I prayed that circle. My point? Each of those properties was once a whisper. That quickening had a net worth of at least $50 million, and it continues to compound interest.

I know some would argue that this promise was meant for Joshua, not me. Trust me, I don't believe in pulling God's promises out of a hat like a rabbit and claiming them out of context. But let me push back a little on this point. This promise wasn't even for Joshua in the first place; it was for Moses. So there is a transitive property at play. Just as God transferred that promise from Moses to Joshua, God transferred that promise from Joshua to me. If that seems like a stretch, remember what 2 Corinthians 1:20 says: "No matter how many promises God has made, they are 'Yes' in Christ." If you're in Christ, all of God's promises belong to you. Each one has your name on it, and the Spirit will quicken different promises at different times. It's one of the ways God whispers.

When Christ returns, the Spirit of God will quicken our earthly bodies. Bodies that are buried six feet deep will be unearthed, and those that have been cremated will rematerialize. But He quickens in more ways than one. Sometimes it's a thought that fires across our synapses. Sometimes it's a prompting to step up, step in, or step out in faith. Sometimes it's speaking the right word at the right time. And sometimes it's a verse of Scripture that jumps off the page and into our spirits.

The psalmist said, "Quicken thou me according to thy word."[17] That word *quicken* is repeated no less than eleven times in the King James Version of Psalm 119. When the Bible says something more than once, we ought to listen to it at least twice.

This may be a little grotesque, but let me paint a picture in a way you probably won't forget. I was channel surfing recently when I came across a rerun of *Mission: Impossible III,* starring Tom Cruise, who plays the role of Impossible Missions Force agent Ethan Hunt. I landed there right when a micro-explosive device was shot through his nose and implanted in his brain. Sorry, that's the grotesque part. And this is a crude example. But the quickening of the Holy Spirit is like a truth bomb that gets implanted in your mind, your heart, and your spirit. When you hide His Word in your heart, you never know when the Spirit of God will make it go off. And that's a good thing!

Here's how it works for me. I usually open my Bible to wherever I left off in my reading plan. I start reading and keep reading until I come to a verse that gives me cause to pause. Sometimes I find the text confusing, so I'll do some additional research. Sometimes I find the text convicting, which leads to confession. And sometimes the text sparks a prompting that I pray into.

One minor caution at this point. Some people employ a flip-and-point approach to the Bible. It's like the guy who was looking for a little inspiration, so he flipped his Bible open and pointed to the verse that says "[Judas] went away and hanged himself."[18] That wasn't very inspiring, so he tried it again. The next verse he flipped to said "Go and do likewise."[19]

I would highly recommend a more methodical approach to the Bible. Why not download a reading plan from YouVersion and read it cover to cover? I'd even recommend a new translation every few years to keep the Word fresh. One way or another, get into God's Word so His Word gets into you. Then the Holy Spirit can quicken it when and where and how He wants.

Deeper Than Cortex

At the age of just twenty-eight, Denny McNabb suffered arrhythmic heart failure. He was resuscitated, but ten minutes without oxygen caused irreparable brain damage. The associate director of East Central Illinois Campus Life lost his memory and with it his history and personality. Denny came out of a coma thirty days later, but he didn't recognize family or friends. He repeated the same question over and over. And his brain became like Teflon; nothing seemed to stick.

My friend and spiritual father, Dick Foth, had an appointment scheduled with Denny the day of his heart attack. That appointment turned into months of hospital visits and some agonizing questions. Chief among them was, how could God let this happen? One day Dick took out his frustration on a hospital elevator, almost breaking his hand. That's when he heard God's gentle whisper: *Dick, I can handle any question you ask Me. You just don't have a large enough frame of reference to handle the answer.*

We'll dive deeper into some of those difficult questions when we explore the language of pain, but it's worth citing something C. S. Lewis said: "Can a mortal ask questions which God finds unanswerable? Quite easily, I should think. All nonsense questions are unanswerable. How many hours are there in a mile? Is yellow square or round? Probably half the questions we ask—half our great theological and metaphysical problems—are like that."[20]

What Lewis meant, I think, is that our questions are often the wrong questions because they are based on such a small frame of reference. You and I aren't smart enough to ask the right questions because we think in finite categories.

About six months after the heart attack, Dick was visiting Denny in the hospital. On a spur of the moment or a spur of the Spirit, he said, "Denny, do you remember this? 'For God so loved the world that he gave his only begotten Son' . . . " Dick stopped quoting midverse. Denny, who couldn't remember a thing, got a faraway look in his eyes. Then he finished the sentence: ". . . that if I believe in him, I won't die anymore."[21] Dick could hardly believe his ears. He said, "Do you remember this?" and started singing, "Jesus loves me this I know for the Bible tells me so."[22] Denny picked it up on key and sang it all the way to the end.

Dick started weeping in that hospital room as the Lord impressed upon him a simple yet profound truth: the spirit of man is deeper than the cortex of the brain. And even when the cortex of the brain is damaged, the Spirit of God can still commune with us. Perhaps that's what the writer of Hebrews was saying: "Sharper than any double-edged sword, it penetrates even to dividing soul and spirit, joints and marrow."[23]

Nearly two decades later Dick was telling that story during a chapel service at Gordon-Conwell Theological Seminary. At the end of the service, a young seminarian came running up to him. He said, "I'm an intern at a local church, and this past week I was sent to a nursing home to see a Mrs. Fredericks." Mrs. Fredericks was well into her nineties, suffering from severe dementia. She would lie in her bed, facing the wall for hours on end and babbling nonsense syllables.

That's how the seminarian found her when he went to visit her. No amount of conversation seemed to break into her consciousness, so the seminarian told her that he was going to leave after praying. That's when Mrs. Fredericks rolled over and said, "Young man, before you go, I want to say something." She began to quote Psalm 119, the longest psalm in the Bible. He quickly turned to the psalm in his Bible to follow along. Mrs. Fredericks quoted all 176 verses, word for word. Then she rolled over and began babbling again.

I don't fully understand why Denny suffered a heart attack in his twenties or why Mrs. Fredericks suffered dementia in her nineties, and we won't sidestep the language of pain. It's a difficult language to discern, but it's a language Jesus knew by broken heart. We'll double back to pain, but let me zero in on this: although we may never get to the bottom of the Bible, the Bible does get to the bottom of us. It penetrates the soul and spirit; it divides joints and marrow. And like a spiritual sonogram, it reveals the thoughts and attitudes of the heart.

The Word of God is longer than the longest memory and stronger than the strongest imagination. It's also deeper than the cortex of the brain. But we must do what the psalmist himself did: "Thy word have I hid in mine heart, that I might not sin against thee."[24]

Reframe

In *The Voyage of the Dawn Treader*,[25] there is a fantastic scene where a painting of a ship on the high seas literally comes to life. A very irksome boy named Eustace Scrubb is badgering his cousins Lucy and Edmund for their silly belief in a place called Narnia when the water from the painting starts flooding the room.

Instead of entering Narnia through a wardrobe, as they had done before, the children enter through the picture frame. It is their portal to a very different reality, a world called Narnia and a lion named Aslan. The picture frame reframes what is possible. The picture frame reframes who they are—boys and girls who become kings and queens.

The Bible is our picture frame. It redefines possibility: "I can do all things through Christ who strengthens me."[26] It reframes reality: "No eye has seen, no ear has heard, and no mind has imagined what God has prepared for those who love him. But it was to us that God revealed these things by his Spirit."[27] And it reminds us of who we really are: "as many as received Him, to them He gave the right to become children of God."[28]

I'm afraid that for some the Bible is like a painting that hangs on the wall. We occasionally give it a glance, but it's nothing more than a pretty picture to look at. It's as static as the status quo. Why? Because all we do is read it. We don't *do* it. The Bible comes alive only when we actively obey it.

The Word of God is as powerful as the four words "Let there be light,"[29] which are still creating galaxies! The Word of God is as powerful as one word, *Ephphatha,* which is opening deaf ears and asthmatic lungs! The prophet Isaiah said that His Word does not return void.[30] The prophet Jeremiah said that God is watching over His Word to perform it.[31] So let's not just read it; let's stand on it. Better yet, let's live it out.

The surest way to get into the presence of God is to get into the Word of God. It changes the way we think, the way we feel, the way we live, and the way we love.

"If you abide in me, and my words abide in you, ask whatever you wish, and it will be done for you."[32] Whatever you wish? Yes, whatever you wish. But here's the catch: if the Word of God truly abides in you, you won't want anything beyond the boundaries of God's good, pleasing, and perfect will. And I'll detail that idea when we talk about the language of desires. Suffice it to say, the Word of God sanctifies our desires until the will of God is all we want.

God is not a genie in a bottle, and our wish is not His command. Quite the opposite. As we grow in grace, His command becomes our only wish.

The word *abide* is repeated nine times in the King James Version of the fifteenth chapter of John. It's a present imperative verb, which indicates continual action. And it's one of those biblical words that has seventy faces. It means to "be moved"; it's one way the Spirit of God stirs our spirits. It means "to stand still"; it's planting our feet on the promises of God and refusing to back down or back off. It means "to stay overnight." When was the last time you pulled an all-nighter in prayer, in worship, in the Word? And it means "to dwell." God not only wants to take up residence within us; He wants to spend all eternity with us.

Hearing the voice of God starts with quickening. If you want to hear the still small voice of God, abiding is key. And the final key to hearing is doing. Hearing without doing is hearsay at best and hypocrisy at worst. We can and must do better than that.

Lectio Divina

The mind produces a wide variety of brain waves, the most common being beta waves, which oscillate between fourteen and thirty cycles per second.[33] Beta waves are associated with normal waking consciousness, including anxious thoughts and active concentration. If we slow our minds down, we enter a state of relaxed alertness that produces alpha waves between eight and thirteen cycles per second. Those alpha waves are amplified by closed eyes, which might be a physiological argument for praying and meditating that way.[34]

The pace at which we read Scripture is not insignificant. Honestly, I tend to speed-read when I get to verses that cause conviction or confusion. But that's when I need to slow down and listen more carefully. Some truths are comprehended only via contemplation. You have to, quite literally, get on the right wavelength. When you feel like reading quickly, read slowly.

Reading the Bible for breadth is called *lectio continua*.

Reading the Bible for depth is called *lectio divina*.

Lectio divina is an ancient Benedictine practice, and it's one way to discern the voice of God. It involves four steps, or stages: reading, meditating, praying, and contemplating. Lectio divina has been likened to a meal, and I like that metaphor.

Reading is taking the first bite. Unfortunately, that's where most people stop. The second step, meditation, is chewing on words and phrases. Instead of dissecting the Word, we let the Word dissect us. The third step, prayer, is savoring the Word. When was the last time you read the Bible for pure enjoyment? It's prayer that turns discipline into desire; "have to" becomes "get to." And the fourth step, contemplation, is digesting the Word and absorbing its nutrients. That's how the Word gets from our head into our heart.

I wish that hearing the voice of God was as easy as reading, but it's not. It requires meditating, praying, and contemplating. Ironically, it's only as we slow ourselves down that the Holy Spirit quickens us. But there is one more piece to the puzzle.

"Christianity has not so much been tried and found wanting," said G. K. Chesterton, "as it has been found difficult and left untried."[35] You can't just read the Word, meditate on it, pray through it, and contemplate it. You have to *do* it. Until you obey it, you've simply been educated beyond the level of your obedience.

"I wonder what would happen," said Peter Marshall, "if we all agreed to read one of the Gospels, until we came to a place that told us to do something, *then went out to do it,* and only after we had done it . . . began reading again?"[36] I'll tell you exactly what would happen: God's kingdom would come and His will would be done! That's what happens when hearers of the Word become doers of it.

Just do it.

Then see what God does!

6

THE VOICE OF GLADNESS

The Second Language: Desires

Take delight in the LORD, and he will
give you the desires of your heart.

—PSALM 37:4

O n New Year's Day 2014, a British ballerina named Gillian Lynne was
named Dame Commander of the Order of the British Empire. I had
no idea what that means, but it sounded awfully impressive, so I looked it
up. It's one of the highest honors bestowed upon a civilian for a noncombatant contribution to the United Kingdom. Methinks ballet qualifies as
noncombatant.

On her twentieth birthday, Gillian was cast as the soloist in the Royal
Ballet's *Sleeping Beauty,* and she never looked back. She parlayed dancing
into a choreography career that produced the likes of *Cats* and *The Phantom
of the Opera*. Gillian's résumé as a dancer and choreographer is perhaps
unparalleled, but like every other success story, it started out as nothing
more than a single-cell desire.

When Gillian was a schoolgirl in the 1930s, teachers were concerned
that she had a learning disorder because she couldn't sit still. Her fidgetiness
would probably be diagnosed as ADHD today, but that wasn't a consideration
back then. So she was taken to a specialist who listened as Gillian's concerned
mother recounted her eight-year-old's issues. Twenty minutes into the

conversation the doctor asked Gillian's mother for a word in private. As they left the counseling room, he turned on the radio and told Mrs. Lynne to watch. Gillian immediately got up and started moving to the music. The discerning doctor said, "Mrs. Lynne, Gillian isn't sick. She's a dancer. Take her to dance school."[1] And that's what Gillian's mother did.

"I can't tell you how wonderful it was," said Gillian. "We walked in this room and it was full of people like me. People who couldn't sit still. People who had to move to think."[2] It was almost as if Gillian were reborn. And although eight decades have come and gone, the desire to dance is still the driving force of her life.

After sharing Gillian's story in the most watched TED Talk in history, "Do Schools Kill Creativity?," education expert Sir Ken Robinson noted the brilliance of the specialist: "Somebody else might have put her on medication and told her to calm down."[3]

Let me go on the record as saying that I'm eternally grateful for doctors and medicine. Both have saved my life multiple times. This isn't an argument against a doctor's prescription in any way. It's simply an argument for pursuing God-ordained desires.

American psychologist Abraham Maslow may have said it best: "A musician must make music, a builder must build, an artist must paint, a poet must write, if he is to be ultimately at peace with himself."[4] And I'd say not just "at peace" but "at liberty." What's the point in trying to be who you aren't? If you succeed, you is who you ain't, and you ain't who you is. You're actually less like the person God designed you and destined you to be. That isn't succeeding; it's failing. And I, for one, would rather fail at something I love than succeed at something I don't. And it starts with deciphering our desires, the second language of God.

Take delight in the LORD, and he will give you the desires of your heart.[5]

We tend to think of desires in a negative light, but C. S. Lewis had the opposite opinion. "We are half-hearted creatures, fooling about with drink and sex and ambition when infinite joy is offered us."[6] According to Lewis, "Our Lord finds our desires not too strong, but too weak."[7] Some desires are sinful, no doubt. And those sinful desires must be crucified. But God also wants to resurrect them, sanctify them, intensify them, and leverage them for His purposes.

Pure Delight

My niece Ella Schmidgall wanted a dog more than anything in the world. Perhaps more than any little girl ever! For five years she prayed and petitioned and pleaded with her parents for a dog. Ella is incredibly sweet, so how her parents held out as long as they did is a mystery to me. After waiting half her life for a dog, Ella got the surprise of a lifetime on her tenth birthday. Her mom told her to close her eyes as her dad handed her a 3.6-pound Maltipoo puppy named Reece. Ella started sobbing uncontrollably. I know this because her mom filmed it for the extended family. I don't know if I've ever seen anyone more overcome with unspeakable joy!

Ella's reaction is my definition of delight.

Seven times in the book of Genesis, God steps back from the canvas of His creation and admires His handiwork and sees that it is good.[8] It's the Almighty's first reaction to His creation. It's the first recorded emotion that God expresses. The word *good* comes from the Hebrew word *tob*.[9] It's joy unspeakable. It's pure delight.

That first emotion sets the tone, sets the bar. God delights in what He does, and He wants nothing less for us. He wants us to delight in His creation. He wants us to delight in one another. And above all, He wants us to delight ourselves in Him.

The first tenet of the Westminster Shorter Catechism says "Man's chief end is to glorify God, and to enjoy him forever."[10] We fully subscribe to the first half, but I'm not sure we fully appreciate the significance of the second half. How much do you enjoy God? Enjoy His Word? Enjoy His presence? Sure, spiritual disciplines usually start out as disciplines. But sooner or later those disciplines turn into desires if you delight yourself in the Lord.

Tell me how much you enjoy God, and I'll tell you how spiritually mature you are. The last thing God wants is for His Word to feel like a chore. Do you read it for enjoyment? If not, you're reading it wrong. Sometimes His Word convicts us of sin, which causes a twinge of guilt, but that's the first step in seeking forgiveness and finding grace. And that always leads to greater joy. Obeying God is our greatest joy, our highest privilege! Loving God with all our strength certainly requires labor, but it should be a labor of love.

Seek First

When I was in seminary, there was a distinct moment when I felt called to write. I was praying in the chapel when the still small voice whispered, *Mark, I've called you to be a voice to your generation.* The irony is that I had just taken a graduate assessment that showed a low aptitude for writing.

Writing is not a natural gifting, but God compensated for that by giving me a strong desire to write. And trust me, it takes a ton of desire to meet deadlines. Sometimes your desires will line up with your talents, and that's where you're doubly dangerous to the Enemy! But God also calls us to do things that are outside our skill sets, requiring tremendous dependence upon His help.

At first my desire to write expressed itself as a voracious appetite to read. As I already mentioned, I read very few books before my senior year of college. But once I felt called to write, I knew I needed to read. And I spent every spare minute and every spare dollar doing it. I read three thousand books before I wrote one.

I have no doubt that God conceived that desire within me. And I write for one reason: I'm called to write. When I sit down at my computer, I take off my shoes because I'm on holy ground. And I don't just type with the keyboard; I worship God with the twenty-six letters of the English alphabet. I've written fifteen books over the past decade, and each one is an echo of that one whisper.

In the Sermon on the Mount, Jesus revealed a supernatural sequence that is inviolable. He said, "Seek first his kingdom and his righteousness, and all these things will be given to you as well."[11] I'm afraid many of us read this backward. We want everything the world has to offer, and then we'll seek God. But that isn't the way it works. You can't seek God second or third or tenth and expect Him to give you the desires of your heart.

Seeking God first is delighting yourself in the Lord.

Seeking God first is giving Him the first word and the last word.

Seeking God first is making sure His voice is the loudest voice in your life.

In the apostle Paul's words, "I consider everything a loss because of the surpassing worth of knowing Christ Jesus my Lord."[12] Then and only then will God speak to us in the language of desires. He'll change our desires, intensify our desires, and upload new desires within us. Those desires actually become spiritual compasses by which we navigate the will of God.

The Voice of Gladness

On the morning of July 11, 1924, Eric Liddell was preparing to run the four-hundred-meter race at the Paris Olympics. Liddell had withdrawn from the hundred-meter competition, a race he was favored to win, because he refused to run on a Sunday. As he prepared for the four-hundred-meter race, which was not his strongest event, he was handed a slip of paper with a paraphrase of 1 Samuel 2:30: "Those who honour me I will honour." Despite drawing the outside lane, the "Flying Scotsman" broke the Olympic and world records with a time of 47.6 seconds and won the gold medal.[13]

In the 1981 Oscar-winning film *Chariots of Fire,* Eric's sister doesn't understand his devotion to the track and tries to convince him to give up running and move to China. He eventually went and served there as a missionary for eighteen years.[14] But he also believed that God was the One who gave him the desire to run. "[God] made me fast," explained Eric. "And when I run I feel His pleasure."[15]

Hold that thought.

A few centuries ago there was a litmus test within the church to determine whether or not something was sinful: "Did you take pleasure in it?" If you did, it was a sin. What a terrible test. God Himself would fail that test in the first chapter of Genesis. The psalmist went so far as to say, "At your right hand are pleasures forevermore."[16] That doesn't sound like a cosmic killjoy! That sounds more like Christian hedonism.[17] In John Piper's words, "God is most glorified in us when we are most satisfied in Him."[18]

Pleasure isn't a bad thing. It's a gift from God. When did we start believing that God wants to send us to places we don't want to go to do things we don't want to do? Sure, taking up our cross involves sacrifice. But when we delight ourselves in the Lord, God will give us the desire to do whatever He's called us to do, no matter how difficult it is.

I've had many conversations with church planters over the years, and one of the common questions they wrestle with is where to plant a church. Many of them have done demographic studies, and that's due diligence. But I always ask the desire question: "Where do you most want to live?" That question often results in a quizzical look, so I double down. "Where do you *want* to raise your family? Do you prefer the city, the suburbs, or the country? Do you want to live by family or get as far away as you can? Are you a mountain person or a lake person? West Coast? East Coast? No coast?" The reason I ask those questions is that I believe church planters will be most successful in places where they really want to live. Seems simple enough, doesn't it? But what makes it difficult is that we're more in touch with others' expectations than our own desires.

Some of us have no idea what we want, because we sacrifice our desires on the altar of other people's expectations. We settle for "should." We settle for "have to" instead of "want to." And then we wonder why we don't feel the joy of the Lord. It's because we're listening to the wrong voices.

Frederick Buechner noted the challenge of choosing the right voice to listen to in his book *Wishful Thinking*. Buechner cited three default settings: society, the superego, and self-interest. If we don't turn them down or tune them out, those become the loudest voices in our lives. Society bombards us with its messages all day, every day. Billboards, commercials, click ads, and social media are the tip of the iceberg. Superego has the loudest voice. And self-interest is not easily tuned out. If you give those voices your ear, you'll conform to the pattern of the world around you.[19]

Buechner then flipped the script and revealed a litmus test I've learned to love. "The voice we should listen to most as we choose a vocation is the voice that we might think we should listen to least, and that is the voice of our own gladness. What can we do that makes us the gladdest? . . . I believe that if it is a thing that makes us truly glad, then it is a good thing and it is our thing."[20]

I might even add, it's a God thing.

If there is a lesson to be learned from Eric Liddell's life, it's probably the same as the principle proposed by Frederick Buechner: listen to the voice of gladness. When we do, the track becomes every bit as much a mission field as China. And you can fill in the blank with whatever you feel called to.

Sweet Spot

Talent or passion? Which is more important when it comes to professional success? You might be tempted to think it's talent, but an eleven-year study led by Dr. Daniel Heller would argue otherwise. The study surveyed 450 elite musical students and found that, over time, passion trumps talent. It was the students' passion for music that inspired greater risks and gave them the intrinsic motivation to persist in the face of adversity. At the end of the day, passion wins the day.[21]

Life is too short not to love what you do, so do what you love. The key is finding the place where gifts and desires overlap. God-given gifts are what we're best at. God-ordained desires are what we're most passionate about. And the place where those gifts and desires overlap is the sweet spot.

We have different gifts, according to the grace given to each of us. If your gift is prophesying, then prophesy in accordance with your faith; if it is serving, then serve; if it is teaching, then teach; if it is to encourage, then give encouragement; if it is giving, then give generously; if it is to lead, do it diligently; if it is to show mercy, do it cheerfully.[22]

The apostle Paul exhorted us to use our God-given gifts in the pursuit of God-ordained desires. And he identified three traits that should define us as Christ followers: generous, diligent, and cheerful. No matter what you do, these three adjectives ought to apply.

The word *generously* comes from the Greek word *haplotes*.[23] It's going above and beyond the call of duty. It's the extra mile. The word *cheerfully* comes from *hilarotes*,[24] which means whistling while we work. It's an A-game attitude. And the word *diligently* comes from the Greek word *spoude*.[25] It's having an eye for excellence, attention to detail. It's showing care and conscientiousness in everything we do. It hints at continual improvement. But there is a nuance that is easily overlooked. Diligence means delighting in what we do. And when we do that, everything we do is transformed into an act of worship.

Martin Luther once observed, "The Christian shoemaker does his duty not by putting little crosses on the shoes, but by making good shoes, because God is interested in good craftsmanship."[26] Amen to that. And speaking of good craftsmanship, essayist Dorothy Sayers once said, "No crooked table legs or ill-fitting drawers ever, I dare swear, came out of the carpenter's shop at Nazareth."[27]

Diligence is doing what you do with an extra measure of excellence.

Diligence is doing what you do with an extra measure of love.

Many years ago I was part of a mission team that helped build a Teen Challenge center in Ocho Rios, Jamaica. I know that doesn't sound like much of a sacrifice, but Jamaica's not all blue oceans and beautiful beaches. Our team worked from sunup to sundown building a ministry center where drug and alcohol addicts could find freedom in Christ. One task was sanding concrete walls to prepare them for painting, but we didn't have a sander. We had to use concrete blocks to scrape the concrete walls, and that sound might be worse than fingernails on a chalkboard. A few hours into it, my shoulders were aching and my nerves were frayed. That's when I heard God's whisper above the sound of the concrete on concrete: *Mark, this is music to My ears!*

At the end of the day, I was absolutely exhausted. But there was a sense of satisfaction unrivaled by any worship service I'd ever experienced. I felt as though I had loved God with all my strength. And when we do that, our energies turn into melodies in God's ears.

412 Emotions

Among the most amazing parts of the human brain are the amygdalae, the almond-shaped clusters of nuclei located within the temporal lobe. Despite amazing advances in neuroscience and neuroimaging, the amygdalae remain quite mysterious. What we do know is that they are the seat of emotion and are intimately involved in decision making and memory making. As a general rule of thumb, stronger emotions result in tougher decisions and longer memories.

Emotions are the subject of much controversy, but they fall into two basic categories: negative and positive. One is vital to surviving, and the other is vital to thriving. Negative emotions, such as fear, keep us out of trouble. Positive emotions, such as hope, get us out of trouble. And it's more than an attitude issue; it's a spiritual issue. Negativity can keep us out of the Promised Land and cost us forty years.[28]

Robert Plutchik, professor emeritus at the Albert Einstein College of Medicine, has identified eight basic emotions: joy, trust, fear, surprise, sadness, disgust, anger, and anticipation.[29] The emotion annotation and representation language (EARL) suggests forty-eight basic emotions.[30] And Professor Simon Baron-Cohen of the Autism Research Centre at the University of Cambridge has identified 412 emotions with corresponding facial expressions.[31]

No matter how many emotions we have, each one is a function of the amygdalae and a facet of God's image and, I would argue, a gift from God. Obviously, that gift must be sanctified and stewarded, as anything else does.

When I was in grad school, one of my professors posed a thought-provoking question: "What makes you cry or pound your fist on the table?" In other words, what makes you sad or mad? Those emotions serve as both cues and clues. I would add glad to mad and sad. Those three emotions help us discern the voice of God. I know that emotion gets a bad rap when it comes to decision making, and I'm not suggesting we let unbridled emotion take the wheel. But emotion is a great backseat driver if we're delighting ourselves in the Lord.

To ignore those emotions is to ignore God's voice. God speaks through our tears—tears of sadness and tears of joy. Isn't that how Nehemiah identified his sweet spot? When he heard that the wall of Jerusalem was in disrepair, he cried. Tears are clues that help us identify God-ordained desires. So does righteous indignation. If we don't get mad at injustice, then our emotions aren't fine-tuned to the heavenly Father. Those emotions must be channeled in the right way, but without them, evil goes unchecked. Our hearts should break for the things that break the heart of God, but they should also skip a beat. Whether it's the voice of sadness, anger, or gladness, don't ignore those emotions. God is speaking to you through them.

Competitive Streak

When I started pastoring, I struggled with an inferiority complex. It reared its ugly head whenever I got around other pastors because I felt so insignificant by comparison, and the key word there is *comparison*. No one wins the comparison game. It only leads to one of two things: pride or jealousy. And both of those things will eat us up from the inside out. I cringed whenever I was asked how large our church was. I felt a little like Saul when he heard the people singing, "Saul has slain his thousands, and David his tens of thousands."[32] In my case we had only dozens in our church!

That inferiority complex was compounded by my being as competitive as they come. I hated losing Candy Land to my kids! It was that competitive streak that helped me overachieve as an athlete, landing first-team All-American honors my senior year of college. I better mention that it was the NCCAA, not the NCAA. The extra *C* stands for Christian, so don't be too impressed. But when my basketball career ended, I didn't have an outlet for those competitive juices. I started out in ministry shortly thereafter, and my competitive streak got the best of me by bringing out the worst in me. It got so bad that I asked God to kill it, but He rebuked my request. It wasn't an audible voice, but God said in no uncertain terms, *I don't want to kill it; I want to sanctify it for My purposes.*

Remember what the apostle Paul did when he was deeply distressed by the idolatry he saw in Athens? He didn't boycott the Areopagus, did he? He walked in, went toe to toe with some of the greatest philosophical minds in the ancient world, and competed for the truth. Paul wasn't one to back down from anyone or anything. He had a sanctified competitive streak, and it was coupled with a sanctified stubborn streak.

It was Paul who said, "Do nothing out of selfish ambition."[33] That's where most of us stop, but that's half the battle. God doesn't just want to kill selfish ambition; He wants to amplify godly ambition. The difference is simply this: Whom are you doing it for?

There is a fine line between "Thy kingdom come" and "my kingdom come." If we cross that line, God will withdraw His favor faster than we can say *sin*. In God's kingdom if we do the right things for the wrong reasons, we don't even get credit. It's all about motives, and the only right reason is God's glory. We're all driven by too much selfish ambition, but none of us has nearly enough godly ambition. You can't have too much ambition when it comes to the things of God.

I try to live by Michelangelo's maxim "Criticize by creating."[34] Instead of complaining about what's wrong, we're called to compete for what's right. How? By writing better music, producing better films, starting better businesses, drafting better legislation, and doing better research. And doing it for God's glory!

Caution Signs

The language of desire is difficult to discern because we have mixed motives, and our ability to deceive ourselves is infinite. Although I believe that God uses emotion to guide us, it's easy to get derailed by emotion. Here are a few hard-earned lessons I've learned along the way. Think of them as caution signs.

First, *check your ego at the door.*

You have to put your ego on the altar every single day. If you don't, you'll fall into the comparison trap. And you won't accomplish much for the kingdom because it'll be about you. Did you know that you can be doing the will of God and God can oppose it? I know that sounds wrong logically and theologically, but it's true. "God opposes the proud."[35] Having pride is letting ego have the loudest voice. And attempting to do God's will in a spirit of pride is two steps forward, three steps back.

Second, *if you want it too much, you might want it for the wrong reasons.*

I know that sounds contradictory, so let me explain. If you want something too much, it's often an indicator that you're not ready for it. Why? Because it's become an idol in your life. An idol is anything you desire more than God, and that includes God-given dreams and God-ordained callings. I've had to die to a few of those desires. And when I put them on the altar, I've found that He sometimes gives them back.

Third, *emotion is a great servant but a terrible master.*

Generally speaking, don't make decisions when you're in an emotional frenzy or funk. That's how you get tattoos in the wrong places. That's when you say things and do things you'll regret. And that's where the ninth fruit of the Spirit is so critical.[36] Actually, I think self-control is listed last because it takes the longest to cultivate. As the emotional gatekeeper, it keeps the other emotions in check.

When Abraham Lincoln was upset with someone, he had a habit of composing what he called a "hot letter." It was a cathartic exercise, putting all his anger and frustration on paper. Then after his emotions had cooled down, he would write "Never sent. Never signed."[37] In psychology that's called a pattern interrupt. It's the difference between reacting and responding. And it's not a bad way of putting James 1:19 into practice: "Be quick to listen, slow to speak and slow to become angry."

Fourth, *one key to discerning whether a desire is God ordained is deciphering whether it waxes or wanes over time.*

Sometimes you have to sleep on it or, better yet, fast on it. Give it some time and see if the desire gets stronger or weaker. If you're delighting yourself in the Lord and that desire passes the test of time by waxing stronger, there is a greater likelihood it's a good thing and a God thing.

And fifth, *a little emotional intelligence goes a long way.*

According to science journalist Daniel Goleman, only 20 percent of the factors that lead to vocational success is related to intelligence quotient.[38] The other 80 percent is related to emotional intelligence, which Goleman defines as "the ability to identify, assess, and control one's own emotions, the emotions of others, and that of groups."[39]

Emotional intelligence is like a sixth sense. And although it's difficult to define, Jesus set the bar. No one could read a room like Jesus. No one was more in tune, more in touch with others. He anticipated the objections of the Pharisees and cut them off at the pass with some brilliant questions. He also discerned the desires of those who were hurting, and He offered healing.

Remember that conference I spoke at in England, the one where they prayed, *Come, Holy Spirit*? What I didn't mention was that I spoke right after the archbishop of Canterbury, Justin Welby. I felt like getting up and saying, "What he said!" and then sitting down. One statement he made has had a profound impact on me, and I've found myself quoting it often ever since. The archbishop said, "Emotional intelligence is a wonderful adjunct faculty to the gifts of the Spirit." It's not enough to exercise spiritual gifts; one must exercise them with a measure of emotional intelligence, or they can actually do more emotional harm than good.

Again, emotion is a gift from God. And as we grow in a relationship with Him, so does our emotional awareness and emotional intelligence.

They express themselves as empathy for others, and that often results in supernatural synchronicities.

Nonconformity

When I was in the sixth grade, I wore a neon-pink Ocean Pacific shirt to school one day. Big mistake! I was pretty popular in junior high, and I was one of the biggest kids in my class. It didn't matter. I was teased mercilessly. Even my best friends betrayed me that day.

Can you guess how many times I wore that shirt? Exactly once. Why? Because I didn't want to subject myself to that kind of ridicule ever again. The modus operandi in junior high is fitting in, and most of us give in to it for the rest of our lives. We become conformists at all costs. And the cost is a person's unique personality, individuality, and identity. You can call it peer pressure or groupthink, but the Bible calls it conformity.

> Do not conform to the pattern of this world, but be transformed by
> the renewing of your mind.[40]

That's one of the hardest commands in Scripture because our culture is so good at conditioning us according to its values. Did you know that you're exposed to approximately five thousand advertising messages every day?[41] It doesn't seem like it, does it? That's evidence of how good our culture is at it. And we have to fight it.

Not many people sell their souls to the devil, but many of us sell our souls to the culture. Instead of defining success for ourselves, we let the culture define it for us. Instead of daring to be different, we conform to the pattern of this world. Why? We let our culture have the loudest voice.

Nonconformity feels like driving the wrong way on a one-way street in rush-hour traffic. But that's the only way to become who God wants us to be. And desire is key.

The word *conformity* is from the Greek word *syschematizo*.[42] It means "to be patterned after or molded by," and it reminds me of the Mold-A-

Rama machine at the Brookfield Zoo in Illinois that has been producing wax figures for more than fifty years now. If I remember right, the options included a pink seal, a green alligator, a brown bear, and a black gorilla. Not unlike those wax figures, most of us get pressed into a cultural mold. The only way to break the mold is to put ourselves on the potter's wheel. Plus, we have to dare to be different.

Divergent Thinking

In the early years of the Head Start program, a study was conducted involving sixteen hundred children who were tested in a wide variety of categories, including divergent thinking. Convergent thinking is the ability to correctly answer a question that doesn't require creativity, just analytical intelligence. Divergent thinking is a very different animal. It's the ability to generate creative ideas by exploring possible solutions.

When asked to come up with as many uses for a paper clip as possible, the average person can rattle off ten to fifteen uses. A divergent thinker can come up with about two hundred.[43] Both convergent and divergent thinking are critical for different kinds of tasks, but divergent thinking is a better predictor of Nobel Prize potential.[44]

In the longitudinal study conducted by Head Start, 98 percent of children ages three to five "scored in the genius category for divergent thinking. Five years later . . . this number had plummeted to only 32 percent. . . . Five years later again . . . it was down to 10 percent."[45]

What happened during that decade? Where did divergent thinking go? And what does that have to do with the language of desires? Here's my take: most of us lose touch with who we really are and what we really want. Instead of following our God-ordained desires in the direction of individuation, the voice of gladness is drowned out by the voice of conformity. And it may start the day you wear a pink shirt to junior high.

We worry way too much about what people think, which is evidence that we don't worry enough about what God thinks. It's the fear of people that keeps us from hearing and heeding the voice of God. We let the expectations of others override the desires God has put in our hearts. The net result? Those desires get buried about six feet deep. Eventually, we forget who we really are.

One of the most thought-provoking questions in the Gospels is this: "What do you want me to do for you?"[46] In one sense the question seems unnecessary, because Jesus asks the question of a blind man. We can all guess his answer, right? He wants his sight, of course. So why does Jesus ask the question? The answer is simple: Jesus wants to know what we want.

If Jesus were to ask the average person walking into the average church, "What do you want Me to do for you?" I'd bet nine out of ten would have a hard time answering that question. Why? Because we're out of touch with what we really want.

If you don't know what you want, how are you going to know when you get it? Maybe it's time to take inventory. What do you want God to do for you? You owe it to Him to answer that question.

Free the Fool

For more than thirty years, Gordon MacKenzie served as creative paradox at Hallmark Cards. His job was helping colleagues slip the bonds of corporate normalcy. He also held creativity workshops at elementary schools. In his book *Orbiting the Giant Hairball,* MacKenzie levels an indictment: "From cradle to grave, the pressure is on: be normal."[47]

When hosting creativity workshops, MacKenzie would conduct informal surveys by asking, "How many artists are there in the room?" In the first grade the entire class waved their arms like crazy. In the second grade about half the hands went up. In the third grade a third of the kids responded. And by the time he got to the sixth graders, only one or two kids would tentatively raise their hands.

According to MacKenzie every school he visited was participating in the suppression of creative genius by training kids away from their natural-born foolishness. Instead of their genius being celebrated and validated, it

was criticized and inoculated. And the voice of normalcy became the loudest
voice in the room.

> There is a fool in each of us, you know. A rash, brash, harebrained,
> audacious, imprudent, ill-suited, spontaneous, impolitic, daredevil
> Fool, which, in most of us, was long ago hog-tied and locked in the
> basement.[48]

Jesus came to set captives free.[49] In other words He came to free the
fool. And not just free the fool but use fools like you and me to shame the
wise.[50]

Salvation is so much more than forgiveness for sin. Jesus wants to set us
free from the psychological straitjacket we've gotten ourselves into, but we
have to dare to be different. We have to walk to the beat of a different drum:
holy desire.

The Bible calls us "a peculiar people."[51] So why are we trying to be
normal? If uniqueness is God's gift to us, then individuation is our gift back
to Him. And it starts with hearing and heeding the voice of desire. And
when God's voice is the loudest voice in our lives, we can dare to be different.

7

THE DOOR TO BITHYNIA
The Third Language: Doors

See, I have placed before you an open door.

—REVELATION 3:8

On December 26, 2004, the third-largest earthquake ever recorded by seismograph[1] occurred deep beneath the Indian Ocean, producing the energy equivalent of twenty-three thousand Hiroshima-type atomic bombs.[2] It registered 9.1-magnitude on the Richter scale, and the shock waves produced tsunami waves more than one hundred feet in height, traveling five hundred miles per hour and reaching a radius of three thousand miles.[3] This deadliest tsunami in history claimed 227,898 lives,[4] but one people group living right in its path miraculously survived without a single casualty.

The Moken are an Austronesian ethnic group that maintains a nomadic sea-based culture. They live on the open seas from birth to death.[5] Their handcrafted wooden boats, called *kabang*, function as houseboats for these sea gypsies. Moken children learn to swim before they learn to walk. They can see twice as clearly underwater as landlubbers. And if there were an underwater breath-holding contest, it would be no contest. But it wasn't any of these skills that saved them from the tsunami. What saved them was their intimacy with the ocean. The Moken know its moods and messages better than any oceanographer, reading ocean waves the way we read street signs.

On the day of the earthquake, an amateur photographer from Bangkok was taking pictures of the Moken when she became concerned by what she saw. As the sea started to recede, many of the Moken were crying.[6] They knew what was about to happen. They recognized that the birds had stopped chirping, the cicadas had gone silent, the elephants were headed toward higher ground, and the dolphins were swimming farther out to sea.

What did the Moken do?

Those who were near the coast of Thailand beached their boats and hiked to the highest elevation possible. Those who were out at sea sailed even farther out to sea. They made it to the deep ocean, where they knew the tsunami crest would be minimalized as it passed them. Burmese fishermen in the same vicinity as the Moken were blindsided by the tsunami and had no survivors. "They were collecting squid," said one Moken survivor. "They don't know how to look."[7] The waves and birds and cicadas and elephants and dolphins were speaking to those Burmese fishermen, but sadly they didn't know how to listen.

According to Dr. Narumon Hinshiranan, an anthropologist who speaks Moken, "The water receded very fast and one wave, one small wave, came so they recognized that this is not ordinary."[8]

One small wave?

Really?

As amazing as it seems, that's all it took for the Moken to recognize trouble. That and an ancient legend that had been passed down from generation to generation about a wave called Laboon, the "wave that eats people."[9] Somehow they perceived this was that wave.

One fascinating footnote. The Moken don't know how old they are because their concept of time is very different from ours. They don't have a word for *when*. They don't have a word for *hello* or *goodbye*. And although we might view that as a logistical liability, it's more than mere coincidence that the Moken don't have a word for *worry* either.[10]

Signs

The Moken are a metaphor. Like these seafaring people who speak the language of the sea, we speak the language of the Spirit. And one of His dialects is doors: open doors and closed doors. In a sense this third language is sign language. Jesus warned against signs and wonders serving as the litmus test of faith,[11] but that doesn't negate their value when it comes to navigating the will of God.

Remember Pharaoh? He ignored ten miracles that were the ancient equivalent of flashing neon signs! How did that work out for him? Ignoring signs is ignoring the God who speaks through them, and we do so to our own detriment.

What if Noah had ignored the forecast?

What if Joseph had disregarded Pharaoh's dreams?

What if Moses had walked by the burning bush without stopping?

What if the wise men had dismissed what the stars were saying?

What if Saul had mistaken his vision on the road to Damascus for an equestrian accident?

If Noah had ignored the sign, he and his family would have died in the flood, and human history as we know it would have ended. If Joseph had disregarded Pharaoh's dreams, two nations would have been destroyed by famine. If Moses had kept walking, the exodus of Israel would not have happened, and the Promised Land would not have been possessed. If the wise men hadn't followed the star, they would not have discovered the Messiah. And if Saul hadn't done an about-face, he would not have become Paul, and half of the New Testament would never have been written.

I know that signs are subject to interpretation, and there is a very fine line between reading them and reading into them. Please don't make decisions based on horoscopes, tarot cards, or palm reading—all of which are forms of divination and false signs. And I wouldn't base your big decisions on fortune cookies either! But we must learn to read signs the way we read Scripture—with the Holy Spirit's help. Make no mistake about it:

God speaks through circumstances. Scripture is our direct evidence, but circumstantial evidence counts too.

The language of doors requires the gift of discernment, which goes beyond intuition based on accumulated experience. It goes beyond contextual intelligence and emotional intelligence. Discernment is the ability to appraise a situation with supernatural insight. It's prophetic perception that sees past problems and envisions possibilities. Simply put, it's picking up what God is throwing down.

Signs Following

Before detailing the language of doors, let me remind you that we don't interpret Scripture via signs; we interpret signs via Scripture. And generally speaking, God uses signs to confirm His Word, His will. Are there exceptions to this rule? Of course. After all, God writes the rules. But the words that close Mark's gospel set precedent: "signs following."[12]

We wish it said "signs preceding," right? That would be so much easier. But that isn't the sequence of faith in Scripture. Consider the parting of the Red Sea and the parting of the Jordan River. Those signs gave the Israelites incredible confidence that God would make a way where there was no way. But Moses had to extend his staff *first*. The priests had to step into the river *first*. Only then did God part the waters. Faith is taking the first step before God reveals the second step.

Our first attempt at church planting was a failure, and I've shared some of those hard lessons in other books, but let me fill in a few of the blanks. In the wake of that failure, I was reading a ministry magazine when I came across an advertisement for a parachurch ministry in Washington, DC. I have no idea why I stopped flipping pages, but that ad arrested my attention. The door to DC opened just a crack. I made a phone call, which led to a visit, which led to a 595-mile leap of faith from Chicago to DC, which led to the past twenty years of ministry in the nation's capital.

That sounds neat and clean, but it was an agonizing decision. Lora and I both grew up in the Chicago area, so it was all we had ever known. Plus,

Michael Jordan was still playing for the Chicago Bulls! Why would we want to move? We had no desire to leave Chicago, but nothing closes a door faster than failure. Actually, it slams the door shut. And sometimes our fingers are still in the doorjamb.

Looking back, I think that failed attempt was the only way God was going to get us where He wanted us to be. It was nothing short of His grace. And I'm as grateful for that closed door as I am for any of the doors He has opened in my life. It was the closed door that led to an open door, and that's how it generally works.

Now here's the rest of the story. Our move to DC was a difficult decision, so I wanted God to give us a clear sign. You know, something simple like a skywriting plane sketching the word *Washington* on the eastern horizon! Part of the reason I wanted a sign was because we didn't have a place to live or a guaranteed salary. But we didn't get a sign until *after* we made the decision to move. Then, and only then, did God give us a sign.

The day we made the decision, I went to our mailbox on the campus of Trinity International University and discovered a postcard addressed to me. The front of the card said, "Your future is in Washington." Not even kidding! Why George Washington University sent me that postcard is still a mystery, but getting it right after making such a huge decision qualifies as a sign following. God didn't just open a door; He rolled out a red carpet.

It's human nature to second-guess difficult decisions, and that's why God is gracious enough to give us confirmations. God knew that I'd experience some self-doubt during the early days of our church plant in Washington, so He sent a postcard. That postcard is a spiritual memento that reminds me of God's faithfulness, even in failure.

Five Tests

When it comes to discerning God's will, I sometimes wish we could just cast lots as the disciples did when choosing Judas's replacement. It'd be a lot quicker and easier than trying to discern God's voice, wouldn't it? But that would take intimacy out of the equation, and intimacy is the end goal.

Discerning the will of God is about so much more than doing His will. Discerning His will is about knowing His heart, and that happens only when you get close enough to hear Him whisper.

Here are five tests I employ when discerning the will of God, the voice of God.

The first test is the *Goose-Bump Test*. The Celtic Christians had an intriguing name for the Holy Spirit. They called Him *An Geadh-Glas*, which means "the Wild Goose."[13] I love the imagery and the implications. There is an element of unpredictability about who He is and what He does. And I can't think of a better description of living a Spirit-led life—it's a Wild Goose chase. We have no idea where we're going much of the time, but as long as we keep in step with the Spirit, we'll get where God wants us to go. That can be a little unnerving at times, but it's awfully exciting too. In fact, it'll give you goose bumps. Or more accurately, Wild Goose bumps!

The will of God should make your heart skip a beat. You certainly have to pass that feeling through the filter of Scripture, but the quickening of the Holy Spirit often causes goose bumps.

I'm certainly not suggesting that you do only the things that get you fired up. Taking out the garbage doesn't give me goose bumps. Neither does doing the dishes. But those jobs have to be done. What I am suggesting is that when you go after a God-sized dream or a God-ordained calling, you should get goose bumps every now and then. The will of God is not drudgery. Remember, if you are delighting yourself in the Lord, then God will give you the desires of your heart. Like a game of hot and cold, those desires will get hotter and hotter the closer you get to God's good, pleasing, and perfect will.

The second test is the *Peace Test*. The apostle Paul said, "Let the peace of Christ rule in your hearts."[14] Does that mean you won't feel scared or stressed? Nope. It simply means this: you know in your heart of hearts that it's the right thing to do. It's a peace that literally passes understanding.[15] It's not just peace in the midst of the storm; it's peace in the perfect storm. Instead of being scared out of your wits, you have a holy confidence against all odds.

The third test is the *Wise Counsel Test*. We don't discern the will of God all by our lonesome. When we try all by ourselves to get where He wants us to go, we usually get lost. My advice? Surround yourself with people who have been there and done that. Surround yourself with people who bring out the best in you. Surround yourself with people who have permission to speak the truth in love. Simply put, seek wise counsel.[16] This test will save you some trials and get you out of others. And because of our infinite ability to deceive ourselves, it's an important check and balance.

The fourth test is the *Crazy Test*. By definition, a God-sized dream is always beyond our abilities, beyond our logic, and beyond our resources. In other words, we can't do it without God's help. In my experience God ideas often seem like crazy ideas. That's how I felt when God originally gave us a vision for a coffeehouse on Capitol Hill. Frankly, we had no business going into the coffeehouse business. But it was just crazy enough to be God.

I don't know what God's will is for your life, and you certainly need to do your homework. But faith is the willingness to look foolish. Noah looked a little crazy building a boat. Sarah looked a little crazy shopping for maternity clothes at age ninety. The wise men looked a little crazy following a star to Timbuktu. Peter looked a little crazy getting out of a boat in the middle of the Sea of Galilee. If you aren't willing to look a little crazy, you're crazy. And when it's the will of God, crazy turns into crazy awesome!

The fifth and final test goes by a longer moniker. I call it the *Released-from and Called-to Test,* and it requires a longer explanation.

One of my spiritual heroes died many years before I was born. Peter Marshall, who immigrated to America from Scotland, served two terms as chaplain to the United States Senate and was pastor of New York Avenue Presbyterian Church in Washington, DC, dubbed "the church of presidents." As it was for Marshall, Washington is my parish. So I found unique inspiration from *A Man Called Peter,* a book and movie about Marshall's life and ministry. But it's how he landed at New York Avenue Presbyterian Church that is particularly instructive.

In 1936 Marshall was asked by the search committee of New York Avenue Presbyterian Church to become their pastor. His response is quite revealing: "I am not yet ready for the responsibilities and the dignities which would be mine as minister of the New York Avenue Church. I am too young, too immature, too lacking in scholarship, experience, wisdom, and ability for such a high position. Time alone will reveal whether or not I shall ever possess these qualities of mind and heart that your pulpit demands."[17] But it was more than humility that kept him from accepting their offer. He felt drawn to the opportunity, but he had just accepted another pastorate and didn't feel released from that responsibility. In other words the timing wasn't right.

The will of God is like a lock with two pins. The first pin is "called to." The second pin is "released from." When you're "released from" a current responsibility but not sure what you're "called to," it can feel like a spiritual no-man's-land. You're not sure what to do next. Until God gives further instruction, I would suggest doing what you heard Him say last.

Marshall found himself in the opposite situation. He actually felt "called to" New York Avenue Presbyterian, but he didn't feel "released from" his current responsibility. A lesser man might have simply jumped at the opportunity, but Marshall maintained his integrity by saying no because it didn't meet the twofold test. It was a year later, after the search committee failed to find another applicant on par with him, that they extended the offer once again. Marshall still felt "called to," and by then he felt "released from," so he accepted their offer, and the rest is history.

The Key of David

One of the promises in Scripture I pray most frequently is Revelation 3:7, and let me note up front that it's a package deal. You can't pray for open doors without accepting closed doors. After all, one usually leads to the other. In a sense, the closed door equates to "released from" and the open door equals "called to."

These are the words of him who is holy and true, who holds the key of David. What he opens no one can shut, and what he shuts no one can open.[18]

I love the iconic opening to the television series *Get Smart.* Maxwell Smart, aka Agent 86, walks through a series of doors to get to the top-secret CONTROL headquarters in Washington, DC. He enters through elevator doors and walks down a corridor with swinging doors, sliding doors, and jail-cell doors before finally entering a phone booth with an accordion door. By my count, Maxwell Smart walks through six doors before getting to where he is going.

I think that's often how the will of God works. We walk through a door and think it's our final destination, but it's actually a door that leads to a door that leads to another door.

Let me have a little fun with this. On a spring day in 2006, I was working on my life-goals list. I was reading a biography of Martin Luther, which prompted Life Goal #106: visit the Castle Church in Wittenberg, Germany, where Martin Luther posted his Ninety-Five Theses.

The very next day I got a phone call from a complete stranger inviting me to speak at an international symposium on the future of the church, in Wittenberg, Germany, on Reformation Day! Are you kidding me? It was one of those moments when you say, "Let me pray about it," followed by a very short pause, followed by a very emphatic "yes!"

You can't base all your decisions on timing, but divine timing is one of the ways God reveals His will. The invitation to speak at that event was a door of opportunity, one of my favorite types of doors. And the domino effect of that one door is difficult to detail, but I'll give it a try.

I took a staff member with me, John Hasler, who eventually moved to Germany and opened our church's café in Berlin with his wife, Steph. That trip was the key catalyst. Without it, I'm not sure the dream would have even been conceived.

I also met an author named George Barna and his agent, Esther

Fedorkevich. Fast-forward two years. I don't think I had a single conversation with Esther after that trip, but she happened to hear a story about Honi the Circle Maker that I shared in one of my sermons, because her brother and sister happened to attend our church. The next day I was wondering if that story might be the beginning of a book when Esther called me and said, "Mark, that's your next book." Esther negotiated the deal for *The Circle Maker,* and she's represented every book of mine since then.

I thought I was going to Germany to go to Germany, but one door led to another door that led to Prachtwerk café, our Ebenezers equivalent in Berlin, Germany. And that door led to another door that led to *The Circle Maker* and every book since.

One of the most mysterious and miraculous ways in which God reveals His sovereignty is by opening and closing doors. Scripture is the key of keys, but there is another key mentioned in this promise: the key of David. It's an allusion to the key that a man named Eliakim wore around his shoulder as a symbol of authority. As the mayor of David's palace, Eliakim had an all-access pass. There was no door in the palace he could not open or close, lock or unlock. Eliakim is a type of Christ, who now holds the key of David. And Jesus is in the business of opening impossible doors and leading us to impossible places. It's one of the ways He whispers.

And for Other Purposes

One of the scariest moments of my life as a leader was the day I got a voice-mail message informing me that the DC public school where our church gathered on Sundays was being closed. I was only two years removed from a failed church plant, and I was afraid it might happen again.

At the time National Community Church was a motley crew. Our income was two thousand dollars a month, and thirty people showed up on a good Sunday. And now we were on the verge of becoming a homeless church. I checked into two dozen options on Capitol Hill, but not a single door opened. Then one day, on a whim, I walked into the movie theaters at Union Station. That's how I discovered that the theater chain had just rolled out a nationwide promotion, called their VIP program, to recruit use of their theaters when they were dark, like Sunday mornings for example. God didn't just open a door; He rolled out the red carpet.

As I walked out of Union Station that day, I picked up a book on its history. The first sentence on the first page I turned to said,

> If, on February 28, 1903, as he signed "an act to provide for a union station in the District of Columbia, and for other purposes," President Theodore Roosevelt could have known what "other purposes" the station would entertain one day, he might at least have sighed before signing.[19]

"And for other purposes."

That phrase jumped off the page and into my spirit. Teddy Roosevelt thought he was building a train station, and he was. But he was also constructing a church building fully funded by the federal government.

For thirteen years the movie theaters at Union Station were home to National Community Church, and it was an incredible run. Not many churches have the amenities that Union Station afforded us—forty food-court restaurants, a parking garage, and a citywide metro system that dropped people off at our front door. Then God did it all over again. I got a phone call in September of 2009 informing me that the theaters were shutting down one week later! We had one week to relocate a congregation that had grown into the thousands.

At first I grieved over that closed door. I honestly wondered if our best days were behind us. But if God hadn't closed that door, I don't think we would have initiated a search for property. Today we own half a dozen pieces of property, valued at roughly $50 million, thanks to a closed door. God has reasons beyond human reason. He has resources beyond human resources too!

Just as we'll thank God for unanswered prayers as much as answered prayers, someday we'll thank God for closed doors as much as open doors. We don't like closed doors when they slam in our faces, and we often don't understand them. But closed doors are expressions of God's prevenient grace.

Sometimes closed doors come in the form of failure. Sometimes closed doors are checks in the Spirit that keep us from walking through the doors in the first place. Either way, God sometimes shows the way by getting in the way.

A Check in the Spirit

On his second missionary journey, the apostle Paul had every intention of going to Bithynia, a Roman province in Asia Minor. He had probably booked nonrefundable fares, but God closed the door. More specifically, Paul was "kept by the Holy Spirit from preaching the word in the province of Asia."[20] That check in his spirit was followed by a vision of a man in Macedonia saying, "Come over to Macedonia and help us."[21]

What makes us think we will discern God's will any differently than Paul did? Sure, we have a fuller revelation of God, thanks in large part to Paul, who wrote much of the New Testament. But Scripture doesn't get us from Bithynia to Macedonia. The God who closed doors then also closes doors now, and to believe anything less is to undervalue the literality of Scripture.

As I mentioned earlier, when I was a senior in college, my whispering spot was the chapel balcony at Central Bible College. Like any college senior staring graduation in the face, I was trying to figure out what was next. That's when I was offered a dream job by a pastor who happened to be my favorite chapel speaker. I was tempted to say yes on the spot. Why wouldn't I accept the offer, my only offer? But as I paced the balcony and prayed about it one afternoon, I felt a strange check in my spirit. Saying no to what seemed a perfect situation on paper was one of the toughest decisions I'd made at that point in my life.

Less than a year later that pastor had to resign because of a moral failure. Would I have survived that situation? I'm sure God's grace would have gotten me through just as it's gotten me through everything else. But God closed the door to "Bithynia" in no uncertain terms—a very clear check in my spirit.

A check in the spirit is difficult to define, difficult to discern. It's a feeling of uneasiness you can't ignore. A sixth sense that something isn't quite right. A lack of peace in your spirit. A check in the spirit is God's red light, and if you don't obey the sign, you might be headed for trouble.

God closes doors to protect us.

God closes doors to redirect us.

God closes doors to keep us from less than His best.

Bithynia was Plan A for Paul, so Macedonia probably felt like Plan B. He probably perceived it as a detour, but it led to a divine appointment with a woman named Lydia, who became the first European to convert to Christianity.[22] And detours like this one were typical of all Paul's missionary journeys. Remember the perfect storm that tossed his ship for fourteen days before it sank off the island of Malta?[23] Was it a shipwreck? Or was it a divine appointment in disguise? How else would Paul have met Publius, the governor of Malta, or healed his sick father?[24]

Coincidence suggests shipwreck.

Providence demands divine appointment.

Remember the old axiom "Don't judge a book by its cover"? The same could be said of our circumstances. What we perceive as detours and delays are often God's ways of setting up divine appointments. And they often start out as closed doors.

Not Yet

Several years ago Lora and I were house hunting on Capitol Hill. Our first home there felt a little like Garbage Compactor 3263827 on the Death Star, which nearly crushed Luke Skywalker, Han Solo, Chewbacca, and Princess Leia as it closed in on them. As our kids got bigger and bigger, our fifteen-foot-wide row house felt narrower and narrower. That's when we found our dream home less than a block away, and it was a whole two feet wider!

We decided to make an offer well below the asking price, but we felt it was a fair offer. And it was our financial ceiling. So our first offer was our final offer, and it functioned as a fleece. With the real-estate market lagging and the house's time on the market mounting, we thought we'd get a contract. We thought wrong. The seller did not accept our offer, and as much as we wanted the house, we took it as a sign to walk away. We were so disappointed that we stopped looking at homes.

Before I go any further, let me explain what I mean by a "fleece." Our biblical precedent is found in Gideon, who put a wool fleece on his threshing floor overnight.[25] Gideon was uncertain what God wanted him to do, so he attempted to confirm his calling by laying a dry fleece on the ground overnight. He then asked God to keep the ground dry around the fleece but allow the fleece to be wet with dew in the morning. Then he reversed the test, asking God to keep the fleece dry and wet the ground with dew. On both occasions God responded to and graciously honored Gideon's request, confirming in his heart and mind his calling.

There is some debate as to whether Gideon should have done what he did. My opinion? Gideon did it in a spirit of humility, and God honored him with an answer both times. I think fleeces have God's stamp of approval, but let me offer a few warnings and instructions.

First, *test your motives.* If you don't test your motives, you might be testing God. And that's not a good idea. Make sure you're asking for the right reasons. Are you ready to obey, regardless of God's answer? Is the fleece a cop-out? If you're looking for an easy answer without any effort, good luck with that. The driving engine must be a genuine desire to honor God no matter what.

Second, *delayed obedience is disobedience.* Make sure the fleece isn't a delay tactic. If it's a subject God has already spoken on, don't try His patience. Make sure the fleece isn't a substitute for faith. Remember, faith is taking the first step before God reveals the second step. There is a time to seek God's will, but there is a time to act on it too.

Third, *set specific parameters in prayer.* If you don't define the fleece, it's easy to come up with false negatives or false positives. Notice the specificity of Gideon's fleece. And don't discount the fact that it required divine intervention.

Back to our dream home. About a year after our offer was rejected, we were driving by the house we had tried to purchase, and Lora said, "Do you ever feel like that is the one that got away?" We weren't fixating on the house. In fact, we drove by it almost every day without giving it a second thought. But her casual comment must have been a prophetic word, because the next morning there was a For Sale sign in front of it.

Can I state the obvious? Sometimes the signs God gives us are literal signs, like a For Sale sign! Don't overlook the obvious. What Lora and I didn't know is that the house had never sold; it simply had been taken off the market after 252 days. Based on the timing, I had a holy hunch that God might be up to something. Perhaps His *no* a year before was really a *not yet*. So we decided to lay down our fleece one more time.

Despite it being the same owner and the same asking price, we made the same offer, the offer he'd already turned down once before. We didn't want to offend the seller, but we told our real-estate agent that it was our final offer. Not only did the seller accept our offer, but because of a rebound in the housing market, we sold our current home for a lot more money than we would have a year before.

We often think that when God closes a door, that is His final answer. We put a period where God puts a comma. We think it's a *no,* but it's really a *not yet.* Is it easy discerning between the two? Not at all. It's hard to know when to hang on to a dream and when to let go. But here's a rule of thumb: if you sense God saying no, give that dream back to Him with an open hand. That often takes more courage than hanging on. But if God hasn't released you, then keep on keeping on.

Donkey Talk

One of the strangest episodes in Scripture is a talking donkey, and I hope the lesson isn't lost on us. If God can speak through a donkey, He can speak through anything!

Forgive me for even suggesting this, but I wonder if the donkey had a British accent. That's how I read it anyway. "What have I done to you to make you beat me these three times?" asks the donkey.[26] I love how articulate this donkey is! And I love that Balaam responds without skipping a beat, as if this is normal. "You have made a fool of me! If only I had a sword in my hand, I would kill you right now."[27]

This is a sidebar, but if you have a talking donkey, the last thing you want to do is kill it. That talking donkey is your cash cow! Turn it into a road show or get a gig in Vegas! But whatever you do, don't kill your talking donkey!

I love that the donkey is the rational one. "Am I not your own donkey, which you have always ridden, to this day? Have I been in the habit of doing this to you?"[28] The donkey sounds like a trial lawyer recounting the facts to a jury. How does the prophet respond? He's reduced to a one-word admission: "No." And I'm guessing he mumbled it with his head down.

Like Balaam, we get frustrated when something gets in the way of where we want to go. We get frustrated with five-minute delays before getting on airplanes that will transport us at speeds that would have been unimaginable to our ancestors. Simply put, we want what we want when we want it, and usually we want it *now*. But sometimes the obstacle *is* the way! God gets in the way to show us the way.

The angel who stops Balaam in his tracks says, "I have come here to oppose you because your path is a reckless one before me."[29]

The word *reckless* comes from the Hebrew word *yarat*,[30] and it's the ancient equivalent of reckless driving. It's overdriving a car's headlights in the fog. It's driving thirty miles per hour over the speed limit around S curves on the Pacific Coast Highway in California.

Don't be surprised if God slows you down.

Don't be surprised if God gets in the way.

Why? Because He loves you too much to let you go headlong into trouble.

If Balaam's donkey teaches us anything, it's this: God can use anything to accomplish His purposes, and He can do it anywhere, anytime, anyhow.

And He particularly likes using foolish things to confound the wise and weak things to confound the strong.[31] In other words we all qualify!

The Sleeper Effect

John Wimber, a founding leader of the Vineyard Movement, was widely respected for his spiritual authenticity. For most of us, the path to faith is full of twists and turns. But John's journey reminds me a little bit of Balaam's.

In his twenties John was a self-proclaimed pagan. He hadn't given God a second thought his entire life. One day he went to downtown Los Angeles to borrow money from his drug dealer, and he crossed paths with a man wearing a sandwich-board placard that read "I am a fool for Christ." John thought it was the dumbest thing he'd ever seen, dumb as a donkey. When he walked past the man, he noticed that the back of the A-frame sign read "Whose fool are you?" Somehow that sign planted a seed in his spirit.

Before revealing the rest of the story, let me share one of the miraculous ways in which the Holy Spirit works. In psychology there is a phenomenon called the sleeper effect. Generally speaking, the effect of persuasion diminishes over time. That's why advertisers try to seal the deal before a message decays. But there are rare exceptions to this rule, and they remain somewhat of a mystery to researchers. Researchers aren't entirely sure how or why this happens, but the persuasiveness of some messages actually increases over time. I think the gospel is the prime example, and the Holy Spirit gets complete credit. He can harvest seeds that were planted decades ago or resurface ideas in the deep recesses of our subconscious.

Many years after that A-frame incident, a very skeptical John went to a Bible study with his wife. His wife began to cry unexpectedly, confessing her sins to the entire group. He was disgusted by her display of emotion and thought, *This is the most foolish thing I have ever seen. I would never act like this.*[32] That's when he had a flashback to the man with the sandwich board. Before he knew what was happening, John was down on his knees, sobbing and asking God to forgive his sin too.

At the risk of offending someone, I'll admit I'm not a huge fan of billboard evangelism. I think it's far more effective to share our faith in the context of friendship. But let's be humble enough to admit that God can speak through anyone, through anything. Far be it from me to tell God how to do His job. After all, He speaks through donkeys, and He still uses fools like you and me!

The Element of Surprise

A quick survey of Scripture reveals a God who always seems to show up in the right place at the right time. His timing is impeccable, but His methodology is unpredictable. Remember the instructions Jesus gave to the disciples when it was time to celebrate Passover?

> As you enter the city, a man carrying a jar of water will meet you. Follow him to the house that he enters, and say to the owner of the house, "The Teacher asks: Where is the guest room, where I may eat the Passover with my disciples?" He will show you a large room upstairs, all furnished. Make preparations there.[33]

We read right over it, but this sounds like a youth-group scavenger hunt, doesn't it?

And then there are the instructions Jesus gave Peter at tax time.

> Go the lake and throw out your line. Take the first fish you catch; open its mouth and you will find a four-drachma coin. Take it and give it to them for my tax and yours.[34]

This has to rank as one of the craziest commands in Scripture. Part of me wonders if Peter thought Jesus was joking. After all, Peter was a professional fisherman. He'd caught a lot of fish in his life, and I'd be willing to bet that none of them ever had a coin in its mouth. Come on, what are the chances?

Let me make a few observations.

First, *God loves doing miracles in different ways.* God will not be reduced to a formula. Once you think you have Him figured out, He'll throw you a curveball. Trust me, you don't need to tell God how to do what He does. You just need to hear what He says and then obey it. And if you want to experience some wild and wacky miracles, you have to obey the crazy promptings.

Second, *God loves surprising us when and where we least expect it.* When it came to fishing, I bet Peter thought he could teach Jesus a thing or two. After all, he was the professional. The area of our greatest proficiency is precisely where we think we need God the least. Perhaps that's actually where we need Him the most.

Jesus could have provided Peter's tax payment in a much more conventional manner, but it would have been much less awesome. I'm not sure which is crazier, a talking donkey or a fish that spits coins out of its mouth! Either way, these aren't anomalies. They are par for the course, and God is as unpredictable now as He was then.

How do you read the Bible? Do you read it like a history book? Or do you read it like it's living and active? Do you read it as if God has finished doing what He did? Or do you believe that God wants to do it again, and again, and again?

Most of us read the Bible the wrong way, with low expectations. I read it with this core conviction: if we do what they did in the Bible, God will do what He did. Why? Because He is the same yesterday, today, and forever.[35] And I'll take it one step further: we'll do "even greater things."[36]

Do we need to hear His voice any less?

Do we need fewer miracles?

Do we need fewer gifts?

Do we need fewer signs?

Do we need fewer open doors and closed doors?

The answers are no, no, no, no, and no.

May God sanctify our expectations so they're on par with Scripture. May we pray with the same kind of expectancy that Billy Graham did when he visited Epworth Rectory: "Lord, do it again!"

One of two things happens over time. Either your theology will conform to your reality, and your expectations will get smaller and smaller until you can hardly believe God for anything. Or your reality will conform to your theology, and your expectations will get bigger and bigger until you can believe God for absolutely everything!

8

DREAMERS BY DAY

The Fourth Language: Dreams

And these are but the outer fringe of his works;
how faint the whisper we hear of him!

—JOB 26:14

A vanilla shake from Chick-fil-A is one of life's simple pleasures, and driving by without driving through feels like a sin of omission. Why? Because it's not just ice cream; it's Icedream.[1] The vision for "Mor Chikin" traces back to Truett Cathy, but the vision for vanilla has a little longer lineage. It traces all the way back to a twelve-year-old slave boy living on a tiny island in the Indian Ocean.

With more than twenty-eight thousand known species, orchids rank as one of the largest plant families in the world.[2] But only one genus produces edible fruit: the vanilla orchid. We take its flavor and fragrance for granted. Vanilla is the most popular spice in the world, but in 1841 the world produced fewer than two thousand vanilla beans, all in Mexico.[3] And because vanilla was so rare, it was all the rage.

"Francisco Hernandez, physician to King Philip II of Spain, called it a miracle drug that could soothe the stomach, cure the bite of a venomous snake, reduce flatulence, and cause 'the urine to flow admirably.'"[4] Princess Anne of Austria drank it in hot chocolate. Queen Elizabeth I put it in her pudding. And Thomas Jefferson did more than author the Declaration of Independence; he authored the first recipe for vanilla ice cream.[5]

Back to the twelve-year-old slave boy. On the island of Réunion, in the city of Sainte-Suzanne, stands a bronze sculpture of an orphan named Edmond. By classroom standards he was uneducated, yet he managed to solve one of the great botanical mysteries of the nineteenth century.

In 1822 a plantation owner on the island of Réunion was granted some vanilla plants from the French government. Only one of them survived, and nearly two decades later it still hadn't fruited. That was the case everywhere outside Mexico for three hundred years. It wasn't discovered until the late twentieth century that a green bee called *Euglossa viridissima* was a key piece of the puzzle. Without that pollinator, no one outside Mexico could get their plants to flower—that is, until Edmond worked his magic.

Ferréol Bellier-Beaumont was walking his plantation with Edmond in 1841 when he discovered, much to his surprise, that his vanilla vine had produced two beans! That's when Edmond revealed, very matter-of-factly, that he had pollinated them by hand. A disbelieving Ferréol asked for a demonstration, so Edmond gently pinched the pollen-bearing anther and the pollen-receiving stigma between his thumb and index finger. It's the same gesture depicted by the bronze statue in Sainte-Suzanne. The French call it *le geste d'Edmond,* which means "Edmond's gesture."[6]

By 1858 Réunion was exporting two tons of vanilla. By 1867 it was up to twenty tons. And by 1898 it was two hundred tons. Réunion actually surpassed Mexico to become the world's largest producer of vanilla beans.[7] And it all traces back to a twelve-year-old boy named Edmond who hand pollinated a single vanilla vine. From that single vine, a billion-dollar industry was created.

Every dream has a genealogy. It's true of Icedream, and it's true of your dream. All our dreams were set up by those who came before, and we follow suit by setting up dreams for those who come after. So our dreams are really a dream within a dream. We're downlines in dreams that trace all the way back to "Let there be light."[8] Creation was God's original gesture. The Cross is His merciful gesture. The Resurrection is His grand gesture. And He is still accomplishing His plans and purposes via dreams and visions through the working of the Holy Spirit.

The language of dreams is the fourth love language, and it's God's lingua franca. There is no dialect that God speaks more fluently or frequently in Scripture. Whether it's dreams by night or dreams by day, God is the Dream Giver.

It was Jacob's dream at a place called Bethel that changed the trajectory of his life. His son Joseph interpreted two dreams that saved two nations. The prophet Daniel interpreted a dream that saved the wise men of Babylon. The Messiah was saved by a dream that warned Joseph and Mary to flee Bethlehem. Paul had a vision of a man in Macedonia that brought the gospel to Europe. And if you're a follower of Jesus and aren't Jewish, your spiritual lineage traces back to a double vision: Cornelius had a vision of Peter while Peter had a vision of Cornelius.

God speaks in dreams so regularly that we often read right over them. Remember when He offered Solomon whatever he wanted, carte blanche? It was a dream. When Solomon woke up, he asked for a discerning heart, which literally means "a hearing heart."[9] Above all else, Solomon wanted to hear the voice of God. That gesture was the genesis of Solomon's becoming the wisest man on earth.

Right-Brain Imagination

To fully appreciate the language of dreams, we need to learn a little neuroanatomy. Nothing is more mysterious or miraculous than the three pounds of gray matter housed within the human skull. On a grand scale the brain consists of two hemispheres that function like parallel processors. Their functions intersect and overlap, thanks to the corpus callosum that connects them, but the left brain is the locus of logic, while the right brain is the locus of imagination.

Neuroanatomists have mapped regions and subregions responsible for a wide variety of neurological functions. The amygdalae process emotion, as we explored in the language of desires. The parafacial zone, located within the medulla oblongata, governs slow-wave sleep. The inferior salivatory nucleus is activated when you walk into your favorite restaurant. And the left parietal lobe is the reason you're able to comprehend what you just read.

Juxtapose that with the Great Commandment: "Love the Lord your God with all your heart and with all your soul and with all your mind."[10]

Does loving God with all our minds include the medial ventral prefrontal cortex? That's the part of the brain that enables us to find things funny, and the obvious answer is yes! In fact, the happiest, healthiest, and holiest people are those who laugh the most. Long before neuroimaging, the Bible declared that laughter does good like medicine.[11]

God wants to sanctify our sense of humor along with every other facet and function of our minds. What does that look like for right-brain imagination? The full answer would require another book, but the short answer is God-sized dreams. After all, the size of our dreams really reveals the size of our God.

If we believe that God is the One who designed the human mind, what would lead us to believe that He wouldn't speak to us through all its component parts? It could even be argued that every feature unique to the human mind is a facet of the image of God. Sometimes He speaks the language of desires by employing the amygdalae. Sometimes He uses the voice of logic, when logic will get us where He wants us to go. God certainly speaks through the five senses, which link to the parietal lobe. And He speaks through memories of the past and dreams of the future.

I was recently at a gathering where Francis Collins, the director of the National Institutes of Health, shared some preliminary findings from a ten-year study of brain circuitry.[12] Three years into the study, it has produced as many questions as answers. Voice recognition and visual recognition, for example, are more mysterious than ever. So is the way memories are recorded and retrieved. But the greatest mystery of all might be the human imagination.

I subscribe to the school of thought that we steward the brain by learning as much as we can about as much as we can. But I also believe in a

God who dwells in the synapses of the brain and speaks to us at the level of thoughts, ideas, and dreams.

Every thought that fires across our eighty-six billion neurons is a tribute to the God who knit us together in our mothers' wombs. But when we have a thought that is better than our best thought on our best day, it might be from God. That doesn't make it equal with Scripture, but it's a step above a "good idea." Is it easy differentiating between good ideas and God ideas? No, it's not. And again, even what we perceive to be God ideas must be screened by Scripture. But when God gives us ideas that we don't believe originated with us, we must be careful to give credit where credit is due. And it's our job to take those thoughts captive and make them obedient to Christ.[13]

Mental Movie

In 1956 Loren Cunningham was a twenty-year-old student touring the Bahamas with a singing group. One night he got into bed, doubled the pillow behind his head, and opened his Bible. He routinely asked God to speak to him, but what happened next was far from routine.

"Suddenly I was looking up at a map of the world," said Loren. "Only the map was alive, moving!"[14] Loren shook his head and rubbed his eyes, much as Edmund and Lucy must have done when the picture of the *Dawn Treader* came alive. Loren likened it to a mental movie in which he saw waves crashing onto the shores until they eventually covered the continents. "The waves became young people—kids my age and even younger—covering the continents." Loren saw this army of young people standing on street corners, outside bars, going house to house, preaching the gospel.[15]

Loren wasn't sure exactly what the vision meant, but it would turn into one of the largest missionary-sending organizations in the world, Youth With A Mission. More than half a century later, there are more than eighteen thousand YWAM staff members in eleven hundred ministry locations in more than 180 countries.[16]

That type of vision might seem a little unusual for some, but isn't that how God spoke to Ezekiel by the Kebar River or Isaiah after King Uzziah died? The entire book of Revelation is a moving picture recorded by John while he was exiled on the island of Patmos. I'm certainly not suggesting that our dreams are equal to Scripture. After all, those visions are part of the canon. But what makes us think that God doesn't speak through the same mechanism, especially when He said He would? Dreams and visions are evidence that we live in the last days.

> In the last days, God says,
>   I will pour out my Spirit on all people.
> Your sons and daughters will prophesy,
>   your young men will see visions,
>   your old men will dream dreams.[17]

The supernatural by-product of being filled with God's spirit is dreams and visions, and prophecy is part of the package deal too. Not only do we need to discern the voice of God for ourselves, but we also need to discern His voice for others. That's one definition of prophecy, and don't be surprised if it's a mental picture.

Now let me make an important observation. The dreams God gives us are for us, but they're never for just us; they're for everyone who will be affected by and inspired by them. Loren Cunningham would be the first person to say that the dream for YWAM wasn't about him but was about the eighteen thousand staff and countless people who have come to faith in Christ.

If your dream becomes a business, your employees are the beneficiaries of the dream God gave you. And so are the customers who buy your goods or services. That's true no matter what you do. If you're a doctor or lawyer or teacher, you didn't go to med school, law school, or grad school for just you. You went for every patient you'd treat, every client you'd represent, or every student you'd teach.

When I was in seminary, I went to see a theater production called *The Toymaker's Dream,* which profoundly influenced me because of the way it imaginatively recast the Creator as Toymaker. I had no idea who made it until I met the producer, Tom Newman, nearly two decades later and was finally able to thank him. God used that play in a significant way in my life and around the world. It was eventually performed for a combined audience of seventy-five thousand people in the former Soviet Union, including key members of the Young Communist Party.[18] I know that God used this play to create change on a global level, but I feel like a primary beneficiary.

One of my core convictions is that the church ought to be the most creative place on the planet. I believe there are ways of doing church that no one has thought of yet. And as an author and a preacher, I try to say old things in new ways. Those values weren't birthed in a vacuum. They were catalyzed by a wide variety of experiences, one of which was *The Toymaker's Dream*. And that's the beautiful thing about dreams. You never know when or where or who or how your dream will inspire someone else to pursue his or her dream. Only the Dream Giver knows that. But we'll have a lot of people to thank someday for directly and indirectly inspiring our dreams.

Mental Picture

National Community Church is now one church with eight campuses, but that wasn't the original vision. With a failed church plant on my résumé, I was hoping for just one campus! Then God gave me a vision at the corner of Fifth and F Streets NE that changed everything. Not unlike the mental movie God gave Loren Cunningham, I saw a mental picture of a Metro map in my mind's eye. I could envision NCC dotting the map in movie theaters at Metro stops all around the DC area.

When I first had that vision of meeting in multiple locations, *multisite* wasn't even a word. Now we're shooting at twenty expressions by the year 2020, and those expressions include church campuses, church plants, coffeehouses, and dream centers. I'm not sure where we'll end up, but each and every expression has a genealogy that traces its origin back to a whisper at the corner of Fifth and F Streets.

God speaks in dreams, and one of the dialects is mental pictures. I've found that to be especially true when I'm praying for others. That may sound mystical, but I would argue that it's biblical.

After David's affair with Bathsheba, God restored him by sending a prophet to confront him. If the prophet Nathan had been too direct, I wonder if David would have reacted defensively. Instead, God gave Nathan a word picture that functioned like a Trojan horse. The prophet told a story about a lamb, which was no coincidence, given that David was a shepherd long before he was a king. That story bypassed David's defense mechanisms, tapped the part of the heart that only stories can, and resulted in full-on repentance.

Nathan used that word picture for the same reason Jesus spoke in parables. Word pictures take a little more time and a little more effort to construct, but few things are more effective when it comes to speaking the truth in love.

Maybe that's why God speaks in moving pictures and mental pictures.

A Little Crazy

When it comes to daydreams, I've had more than my fair share. When it comes to night dreams, I think I'm below average. I hardly ever remember my dreams, and when I do, they don't make much sense to me. That said, I was recently challenged by my friend Kurtis Parks, who told me about his long-standing habit of asking God to speak to him through his dreams.

Before coming on staff at NCC, Kurtis was traveling and singing at camps and churches while holding down a day job in delivery. When he unexpectedly lost that job, he wasn't sure how he'd make ends meet. Kurtis put it to prayer before going to bed one night, and he dreamed that night that he was leading worship at a church in Charlottesville, Virginia. The next morning Kurtis was awakened by a phone call from the pastor of that church, inviting him to come and lead worship that weekend. Kurtis even led "Salvation Is Here,"[19] the same song he had seen himself leading in his dream. And the honorarium he received was a few dollars more than his monthly mortgage payment. "It was a powerful moment, knowing that God was aware of my anxiety in the awake world and gave me assurance in the dream world," said Kurtis.

We tend to be skeptical of experiences we've never had, and that's especially true when it comes to things such as night dreams. If we aren't careful, we dismiss people as being a little crazy if they experience God in ways we haven't. But maybe we're the ones who are a little too normal. If there is a biblical precedent for God speaking through dreams, why wouldn't we pray for the same experience? Maybe we have not because we ask not.[20]

My wife, Lora, and sister-in-law, Nina, recently spent a week in the refugee camps in Thessaloniki, Greece, with our missionary friends Tony and Jamie Sebastian. During their visit they met a refugee couple who shared their testimony with them. Emmanuel was born and raised in Iran, while his wife, Amanda, is from Kurdistan.

Emmanuel grew up Shia Muslim, so prayer was part of his religious routine. But when he prayed, he felt as if no one was listening. A friend gave Emmanuel a Bible, telling him that Jesus wanted to talk to him, so Emmanuel asked Jesus to reveal Himself if He was real. That is precisely what happened. Emmanuel had a vision of Jesus and heard His voice. His newfound faith in Christ put his life in jeopardy, so he fled his country. That's how Emmanuel met his future wife, Amanda, in Istanbul, Turkey. It was more than love at first sight. God whispered to Emmanuel that Amanda was to be his wife despite the fact that they didn't speak each other's language. The day after they were married, Emmanuel was miraculously able to speak and understand the Kurdish language! No, that's not a typo! It's on par with what happened on the day of Pentecost.

The newlywed couple eventually fled Turkey and traveled by boat to Greece. The trip took longer than expected, and Amanda became deathly ill. One night a light came into their tent in their refugee camp, and Emmanuel heard a whisper that help was on the way. The next day two women showed up, saying God had sent them to help. They got Amanda to a hospital, but the doctors weren't able to solve her symptoms. Then one night Amanda had a vision of Jesus standing by her bed, putting His hands on her head and praying for her healing. When she woke up, her symptoms were gone. The doctors didn't want her to leave, but Amanda checked herself out of the hospital and was immediately baptized. This couple is now in training to be the first Arabic-speaking pastors of a church in Thessaloniki, Greece.

Just an ordinary day at the office, right? Maybe not to us, but miracles like that are happening all the time all around the world. Muslim refugees are coming to faith in Christ via visions, miracles, and the hospitality of Christians. And because many of them don't have Bibles, God speaks through signs and wonders.

This might be an appropriate place for a reminder that God is doing *now* what He did *then*. And maybe He wants to do *here* what He is doing *there*.

Strange Visions

One of the strangest dreams recorded in Scripture is Peter's vision of four-footed animals, reptiles, and birds being let down to earth in a sheet. Then a voice said, "Get up, Peter. Kill and eat." I love Peter's response: "Surely not, Lord!"[21] I'm pretty certain if you're calling someone *Lord*, the two words that should never precede it are "surely not." But I understand Peter's hesitancy. This dream seemed more like a nightmare because it contradicted every Jewish dietary law on the books. Peter must have felt like a vegetarian at an all-you-can-eat Brazilian steak house.

Let me zoom out and make a couple of observations. First, *God-given dreams won't contradict Scripture.* One could argue that this vision was an exception to that rule, but the canon wasn't closed yet. God was outmoding Jewish dietary laws while onboarding Gentile believers, and He accomplished both with one dream. A God-given dream won't take you beyond the boundaries of Scripture, but it will stretch you to do things you didn't know you were capable of even attempting.

Second, *God-given dreams will confront prejudice.* At that point in history, Christianity was essentially a sect of Judaism. The thought of

Gentiles being grafted into Christ was so radical that the dream had to be repeated three times! Sometimes God has to force us outside our comfort zones. We want Him to do something new while we keep doing the same old thing, but it doesn't work that way. His voice challenges the status quo and nudges us in new directions.

Third, *the meaning of dreams isn't always immediately discernible.* If Peter had to process dreams, we probably will too. Some dreams make immediate sense, but others won't make sense for decades. And dreams are like doors: often one leads to another, which leads to another.

Finally, *if you want to establish God's reputation, you might have to risk yours.* Peter took a calculated risk when he entered the house of Cornelius. Technically speaking, it was against the Law. But like Paul, Peter "was not disobedient to the vision from heaven."[22] He preached the gospel, Cornelius repented, and the playing field was leveled between Jew and Gentile.

If you're a Gentile believer, your genealogy traces back to that moment. Actually, it traces back to a double vision, a double whisper. Cornelius acted on the dream God gave him, and then Peter acted on the dream God gave him, and they met in the miraculous middle.

We tend to view stories like this one as anomalies, but shouldn't they be normalities? Just because we have access to the sacred text of Scripture, that doesn't mean we should expect fewer miracles. Scripture ought to fuel our faith for more. If God can use a double vision to set up a divine appointment between an Italian soldier and a Jewish apostle, why wouldn't He do the same for us?

Remember my bravest prayer, the prayer that God would heal my asthma? After I preached that message, a guest approached me and told me about a dream she had the night before. In her dream she laid hands on my lungs and prayed for them, and they were healed. She asked if she and her husband could do what she had done in her dream. Honestly, I was a little wary, because they were complete strangers. But the last thing I want to do is get in the way of what God wants to do, even if it seems a little strange to me. And the reality is, they took a risk even making that request. So I gave this couple permission to lay hands on me, as Scripture instructs,[23] and to pray for healing. I don't know what role that prayer played in my healing, but it's a piece of the puzzle. It was a catalyst for and a confirmation of my healing. It was also a reminder that God works in strange and mysterious ways.

Pure Faith

On April 1, 1908, John G. Lake had a vision of himself being transported to South Africa and preaching. That dream was repeated several times, not unlike Peter's vision. Eighteen days later Lake and his family left for Africa with $1.50 in their pockets. Lake was well aware that it would cost $125.00 to get his family of eight through immigration, which was nearly a hundred times what they had. But he felt as though God had told them to go.[24]

When their family arrived in South Africa, Lake got into the immigration line despite not having enough money to enter the country. That's when someone tapped him on the shoulder and handed him $200.00. The Lakes boarded a train for Johannesburg, but they still had no place to live, so they prayed on the way there that God would provide. When they arrived, they were greeted at the train station by a woman named Mrs. Goodenough, who said that God had told her to give them a place to live.

It's hard to calculate the influence of someone's life, but John G. Lake was an integral part of a revival that swept across South Africa. He later returned to America, where he started forty churches.[25] And perhaps his greatest influence was through a son in the faith, Gordon Lindsay, who founded Christ for the Nations.

Why did God use Lake the way He did? Well, if someone is willing to move his family of eight halfway around the world in response to a vision, God can probably use that person to do just about anything! His willingness to go anywhere and do anything was unparalleled, and so was his hunger for God.

Lake once said, "I believe I was the hungriest man for God that ever lived."[26] It's tough to judge a self-assessment, but I will say this: If you stay humble and stay hungry, there is nothing God cannot do in you or through you. In fact, the humbler you arc, the bigger the dream God can entrust to you, because He knows that He'll get the glory.

One last reminder. The goal of going after a God-given dream isn't just accomplishing it. In fact, accomplishing the dream is of secondary importance. The primary goal is who you become in the process. Big dreams make big people because we have to trust a big God. Nothing keeps us on our knees like God-sized dreams. They force us to live in raw dependence upon God. Without Him, the dream cannot be realized. God-sized dreams force us to lean in a little closer, and that's when God has us right where He wants us.

HIDDEN FIGURES

The Fifth Language: People

We are surrounded by such a great cloud of witnesses.

—Hebrews 12:1

On February 20, 1962, John Glenn sat atop a ninety-five-foot-tall intercontinental ballistic missile at Cape Canaveral. After eleven delays capsule communicator Scott Carpenter finally uttered the famous phrase "Godspeed, John Glenn,"[1] and the Mercury-Atlas 6 blasted off from Launch Complex 14. It reached a velocity of 17,544 miles per hour, orbited Earth three times, and splashed down four hours, fifty-five minutes, and twenty-three seconds later eight hundred miles southeast of Bermuda.[2] John Glenn was an instant hero—the first American to orbit Earth. But even heroes need help. And epic stories often have even better backstories.

The greatest challenge facing NASA wasn't getting a man into space; it was returning him safely to Earth. And that's where Katherine Coleman Goble Johnson entered the equation. Calculating Glenn's reentry into Earth's atmosphere required the brightest mathematical minds, and Katherine was chief among them. But she had to overcome two significant challenges: It was a white world in 1962, evidenced by the bathrooms designated specifically for black employees at Langley Research Center. And it was a man's world. But you can't keep a good woman down.

When it came to calculating trajectories and computing launch windows, no one was better than Katherine Johnson. NASA had purchased their first IBM computer a few years earlier, but John Glenn trusted human computers more than the machine version. In fact, he wasn't willing to take off until Katherine checked the numbers. So John Glenn made a special request: "Get the girl to check the numbers."[3]

I don't want to overstate the facts. Perhaps NASA could have found someone else to verify the numbers, but play along for a minute. If Katherine didn't do what she did, I'm not sure John Glenn would have done what he did. And if John Glenn had not orbited Earth, we wouldn't have shot the moon. And if we didn't land a man on the moon, the Soviet Union would have. And if the Soviet Union had won the space race, they might have won the Cold War.

Here's my point: there are people we've never heard of, hidden figures, who have changed the course of history in ways we're totally unaware of. I'm not sure any of us would even know Katherine Johnson's name if she hadn't been awarded the Presidential Medal of Freedom at the age of ninety-seven.[4] Well, that and an Oscar-nominated film. And Katherine Johnson helped put a man on the moon, for goodness' sake!

Behind every John Glenn, there is a Katherine Coleman Goble Johnson. And that trend is true in Scripture too. Behind Moses, there is Aaron. Behind David, there is Benaiah. Behind Esther, there is Mordecai. Behind Elisha, there is Elijah. Behind Timothy, there is Paul. In the words of English poet John Donne, "No man is an island entire of itself."[5]

Do you know why C. S. Lewis went to church? It's not because he loved the songs. He thought they were "fifth-rate poems set to sixth-rate music."[6] It's not because he loved the sermons. And it's not because he liked the people. He didn't. Lewis went to church because he believed that if he didn't, he would fall into something he called solitary conceit. He knew that we aren't designed to make it on our own.[7]

When we isolate ourselves from others, we become islands unto ourselves. And like Tom Hanks in the movie *Cast Away*, we eventually draw a face on a volleyball, name it Wilson, and start talking to it.

You know why God puts people in our lives? It's not just to overcome solitary conceit; it's also to overcome solitary confinement. He puts people in our lives to keep us humble and to draw out our potential. I like to think of it as human pinball; we bump into different anointings, different giftings, different ideas. Somehow God uses those relational encounters to get us where He wants us to go.

Did you know it took approximately four hundred thousand people to put a man on the moon? It took a twenty-six-year-old mission controller named Steve Bales. It took a twenty-four-year-old computer whiz named Jack Garman, who memorized every alarm code. Then there was Robert Carlton, who was in charge of monitoring fuel consumption. He's the one who, after the module had traveled 240,250 miles, announced that they had only sixty seconds of fuel left to land the module or they'd have to abort. And don't forget Eleanor Foracker, a seamstress who worked for the company that designed the space suits. She and her colleagues got a little nervous when the astronauts started jumping on the moon, but her seams held tight. That's four names out of four hundred thousand, but you get the point.[8] No one shoots the moon alone.

Each of us is a link in the chain of "begats" that started with Adam and Eve. The chain is filled with unsung heroes who won the day and hidden figures who saved the day. We all stand on one another's shoulders. The writer of Hebrews calls this human chain the cloud of witnesses.

Since we are surrounded by such a great cloud of witnesses, let us throw off everything that hinders and the sin that so easily entangles. And let us run with perseverance the race marked out for us.[9]

We all have a cloud of witnesses, and that cloud consists of anybody and everybody who has influenced our lives. It's our family and friends, coaches and teachers, and, I'd like to think, pastors and authors. To believe that any of those people are in our lives by happenstance is to grossly underestimate the sovereignty of God. He wants to use them to speak into our lives, and He wants to use us to speak into theirs.

A Spirit of Timidity

The fifth love language of God is people. Yes, God can speak through a donkey, but more often than not, He uses people. He used a prophet named Nathan to rebuke King David. He used an uncle named Mordecai to exhort Queen Esther. And He used a spiritual father named Paul to encourage Timothy: "God has not given us a spirit of timidity, but of power and love and discipline."[10]

It's a verse to us. It was a prophetic word for Timothy.

It's tough to typecast Timothy, but let me try. I think he was more of a feeler than a thinker, as evidenced by his crying when he parted ways with Paul.[11] A man hug is one thing; crying is next level. And I can't prove it, but I think Timothy struggled with an inferiority complex. I don't know if it was a function of age or a function of personality, but it seems that he struggled with insecurity, as indicated in Paul's letter to the Corinthians: "When Timothy comes, don't intimidate him."[12] Things that make you go *hmmm.*

All of that adds up to Paul's exhortation.

The word *timidity* comes from the Greek word *deilia.*[13] It's the only occurrence of that word in the New Testament, and it means "cowardice." It's the inability to face danger without showing fear. It's a lack of grit. It's a failure of nerve. First-century historian Josephus used the word to describe the ten spies who brought back bad reports about the Promised Land out of fear of the giants. And it's the opposite of a martyr. In other words, a person who denies his faith to save his life.

On that note let me tell you how Timothy died. According to church tradition, he died at eighty years of age trying to stop a pagan parade![14] What happened to timid Timothy? That's not timid at all. Timothy was dragged through the streets and eventually stoned, dying a martyr's death. I think Timothy was done playing the coward, done being intimidated. I think he determined to do exactly what his spiritual father had done: fight the good fight, keep the faith. And I can't help but wonder if this act of courage traced back to one word of exhortation, if Timothy heard Paul's voice above the parade.

If you've tracked with me this far, I think we've built up enough trust for me to speak a word of exhortation: quit using your personality as an excuse! When you use your personality as an excuse, you no longer have a personality; your personality has you.

When God called Jeremiah to be a prophet, he starting making excuses. He said, "I can't speak for you! I'm too young!"[15] And we do the same exact thing, don't we? We're too much of this or not enough of that. But if God is sovereign, then we can't be too young, too old, too timid, or too bad. God cut Jeremiah off: "Do not say, 'I am too young.'"[16]

What parts of your personality have been a crutch?

What excuse do you need to confess?

Abraham was too old.

Moses was too criminal.

Peter was too impulsive.

James was too analytical.

John was too emotional.

Timothy was too timid.

You tell me your excuse, and I'll tell you where God wants to use you. That's how He puts His grace and His glory on display.

The Johari Window

When I was in graduate school, I was introduced to a fascinating matrix on human personality called the Johari window. In case you care, *Johari* is a combination of the names of the two guys who came up with it, Joe and Harry. The quadrants are really four windows into personality and identity.

The first quadrant is the *arena quadrant,* and it consists of those things *you know about you* and *others know about you.* It's your public persona. It's your Facebook feed. It's what everybody knows, everybody sees.

The second quadrant is the *facade quadrant,* and it consists of those things *you know about you* but *others don't know about you*. This is your alter ego. This is who you are when no one is looking. This is the curtain that hides the real Wizard of Oz. The second quadrant is where we fake it to make it, but we're only fooling ourselves. It's why we get stuck spiritually. It's why we hide emotionally.

When I was in kindergarten, I had a crush on a little girl in our church, and it must have been obvious, because my parents said something about it in the main sanctuary with other people present. I can't remember what they said, and I'm sure it was absolutely innocent. I have wonderful parents. But I remember a feeling of shame that I can't quite put into words. When we got home, I locked myself in my bedroom and made a sign that read "I'm never coming out." And I never did. Sure, I came out for dinner. But I never came out emotionally. It took me a long time to admit to anyone that I liked a girl, because subconsciously I was afraid of being made fun of. And that's on me, not my parents. But it became a taboo topic. I hid those feelings, didn't answer those questions, and avoided those conversations.

We all have things we hide behind the facade. We cover it up with a Sunday smile, but it's the deep disappointment we've never fully reconciled and the acute anxiety when we find ourselves in certain situations. It's secret sins we've never had the courage to confess and secret dreams we've never dared to verbalize. The net result is shallow conversations and superficial relationships, and that isn't the abundant life Jesus promised.

The only way out of the second quadrant is confession. And I don't mean just confessing your sins to God. Take it a step further: "Confess your sins to each other and pray for each other so that you may be healed."[17] While you're at it, confess your excuses. And your fears. And your weaknesses. And your doubts.

Confessing our sins to God nets forgiveness, but confessing our sins to each other is a critical part of the healing process. And it's not just for you; it's also for the person you're confessing to. The Enemy wants you to keep your secret a secret; it's an ancient isolation tactic. It's only when we confess our sins to each other that we realize others are also struggling with pride or lust or anger. And now we can actually help each other, challenge each other, and hold each other accountable. Confession gives the other person the opportunity to encourage us, exhort us, and console us.

"If we could read the secret history of our enemies," said Henry Wadsworth Longfellow, "we should find in each man's life sorrow and suffering enough to disarm all hostility."[18] Everyone you meet is fighting a battle you know nothing about—until he or she confesses it, of course.

As I see it, we have two options: an alter ego or an altar ego. Having an alter ego means pretending to be who we're not, and it's absolutely exhausting. The other option is to put our ego on the altar and find our full identity in Jesus Christ. That's how we silence the loudmouth ego. Putting our ego on the altar means accepting God's assessment of who we are, the apple of His eye. And seeing ourselves as anything less than who He says we are is false humility.

The Blind Spot

That brings us to the third quadrant, the *blind spot quadrant,* which consists of those things *you don't know about you* but *others know about you.* This is getting ready to go on stage with your barn door open. You need someone in your life who loves you enough to say what needs to be said: "Zip it up!" This is where we need spiritual fathers and spiritual mothers who have been there and done that. This is where we need friends who have permission to speak the truth in love. This is where we need accountability partners who can call us on the carpet and remind us that we were born for so much more.

At the place where the optic nerve passes through the optic disk, all of us have a literal blind spot. It's approximately 7.5 degrees high and 5.5 degrees wide. We rarely notice our blind spots because our brains are so good at filling in the blanks based on visual clues, but they're also where we're most susceptible to misjudgment, misinformation, and misunderstanding.

One of the first lessons learned in driver's education is to check your blind spot before changing lanes. That's one way to avoid accidents. And what's true of driving is true of life. It's also why the fifth language— people—is so critical. Without the influence of others, we develop blind spots. And those blind spots are spiritual weak spots.

One of the defining moments of my life was the day an intern had the courage to call out the pride he saw in me. At first I was defensive. But when I realized that he was right, I repented. I also made a vow that I'd do my best not to talk negatively about other churches or pastors. I decided to do the opposite, and it's become a mantra around National Community Church: brag about people behind their backs.

Maybe you're more mature than I am, but I generally don't like it when someone says what I don't want to hear. But if it's what I *need* to hear, that's the person I'll thank most at the end of the day. It's been fifteen years since that defining moment, but I'm still indebted to that intern who noticed a hint of pride and loved me enough to tell me.

Remember the voices that deafen us to God's voice? The voice of criticism can blind us to our own potential. But if the truth is spoken in love, the right word at the right time has the power to open our eyes.

We all have unresolved issues and unhealed hurts. We have a plethora of defense mechanisms, conditioned reflexes, and coping strategies that we aren't even aware of. If we've been in intimate relationships with those we trust and they've violated our trust in some form or fashion, it leaves scars. That scar tissue can make it tougher for us to trust the next time. And if we aren't careful, we sabotage ourselves with self-defeating behaviors because we're subconsciously afraid of it happening again.

The only way to overcome those self-defeating dimensions of our personalities is ruthless self-discovery. And it's so much more than self-help. "Without knowledge of self," said John Calvin, "there is no knowledge of God."[19] If done correctly, personality assessments help us discover the way God has wired us. The obvious danger is that we pigeonhole ourselves and others. Or as I've already mentioned, we use personality as an excuse. Let's not do that, but ignorance is not bliss either.

I love StrengthsFinder.[20] As the name suggests, it helps people discover their God-given gifts. But I also value the Enneagram because it helps us identify the deadly sins we are most susceptible to. According to author and pastor Ian Cron, "Each personality's deadly sin is like an addictive, involuntary repeated behavior that we can only be free of when we recognize how often we give it the keys to drive our personality."[21]

There is a healthy and holy manifestation of our personalities, but there is an unhealthy and unholy manifestation too. And there is often a fine line between those two. We need people who are full of grace and full of truth to help us navigate that line and hold us accountable when we cross it.

Consider the Source

The fifth language is the most commonly used, but it's also the most commonly misused and abused. So let me share some hard-earned advice before we get to the fourth quadrant. God speaks through people, but those people are as imperfect as we are. So here's a good rule of thumb: consider the source. An insult from a fool might be a compliment, and a compliment from a fool might be an insult. Either way, you have to consider the character of the person saying it.

In my experience, God speaks to us through friends more frequently than strangers. I'm not saying God can't use someone you don't know to say something you need to hear. He most certainly can, and He most certainly has in my life. But speaking the truth in love is an earned right, and it's the by-product of relationship. The stronger the relationship, the more weight those words carry.

I know far too many people who have been hurt by careless words. That doesn't mean we tune out everybody and stop listening. It just means we better be more discerning. In the words of the apostle Paul, "Weigh carefully what is said."[22] Before you buy what someone is selling, make sure it passes through the filter of Scripture. And don't just consider the person's words; consider his or her character when giving weight to the words.

Now let me flip the script. If you are dialing into the still small voice of the Holy Spirit, there will be moments when God gives you a word to speak into someone else's life. Paul delineated three different types of words: a word of wisdom, a word of knowledge, and a prophetic word.[23]

Sometimes God speaks to us *for us.*

Sometimes God speaks to us *for others.*

One of the greatest gifts you can give someone is not just to pray for that person but also to listen to God for him or her. If you cultivate a prophetic ear, God will give you a prophetic voice. But it comes with a caution: what's true of listening is true of speaking. Jesus said, "Do not . . . cast your pearls before swine."[24] It's the corollary to "consider the source." Simply put, consider the person. If someone isn't ready, willing, or able to hear what you have to say, you're wasting words. If you discern a lack of readiness, you might need to do what Jesus did: hold your tongue. Jesus said, "I have much more to say to you, more than you can now bear."[25] The right word has to be spoken at the right time, or it can actually have the wrong effect.

Prophetic Ear

My spiritual father, Dick Foth, has been preaching for more than fifty years, but something happened recently that had never happened to him before. In the middle of a message, Dick sensed in his spirit that someone was on the verge of an affair that very week. That impression came out of nowhere, and Dick wasn't entirely sure what to do with it. It was a calculated risk, but he figured he better say something. So he interrupted his own sermon and said, "There is someone here who has set themselves up to have an affair. The pieces are in place, and you were planning on making the decision today. Don't do it." After the service a middle-aged man gave Dick a big bear hug. When he did, he whispered, "That was me. Thank you."

Dick is one of the most unassuming people you'll ever meet and one of the nicest too. That word of knowledge was a little out of the ordinary for him, and he'd even say it was a little out of his wheelhouse. But his obedience to that whisper quite possibly altered a family tree for generations to come.

The right word spoken at the right time can echo for eternity, and it starts with a prophetic ear.

I can't imagine him ever introducing himself this way: "Hi, I'm Dick. I'm a prophet." Most of us run away from people who self-identify that way. But let's not shy away from spiritual gifts. We mistakenly think of prophets as oracles who predict the future, but that isn't the biblical definition. It's more forthtelling than foretelling.

By definition, a prophetic word is strengthening, encouraging, and comforting.[26] That doesn't mean it can't be confrontational, but it's always redemptive. And it should be delivered with a gentle spirit.[27]

You may not think of yourself as a prophet, but it's who you're called to become. Jewish philosophers did not believe that the prophetic gift was reserved for a few select individuals. Becoming prophetic was seen as the crowning point of mental and spiritual development. The more people grow spiritually, the more prophetic they become. Moses himself said, "I wish that all the LORD's people were prophets."[28]

One footnote. Just like natural talents, supernatural gifts must be exercised. You're not going to be great right out of the gate, and I know this from personal experience. My first sermons were more pathetic than prophetic. My first "official" sermon was in a country church in Macks Creek, Missouri. That poor church! I was taking a class in eschatology at the time, so I laid out an entire time line for the end times, a time line that changed from class to class. I owe that church an apology in heaven.

I'm a work in progress, and so are you. But don't let inexperience keep you from exercising your gifts. Don't let doubt keep you from exercising your faith. And don't let the fear of people keep you from speaking into their lives, as God leads. My only exhortation is that we do so in a spirit of humility. Let love lead and the gifts follow.[29]

Dick Foth has permission to speak into my life, but he often uses a little disclaimer before doing so. He says something like, "If ten is a word from God and one is a word from Foth, this is a four." Or it might be a two or a five or even a nine. I like that approach because it suggests something supernatural, but it also allows for a margin of error.

The Unknown Quadrant

The fourth quadrant is the *unknown quadrant,* and it consists of those things *you don't know about you* and *others don't know about you.* I call it your soulprint, and it's the truest thing about you. It's your God-ordained passions, your God-given gifts, and your God-sized dreams. It's the potential that can be tapped only in a relationship with the One who gave it to you in the first place.

God knows you better than you know you. Not only did He knit you together in your mother's womb, but He has prepared good works in advance with your name on them.[30] If you want to discover who you really are, seek God.

Author and speaker Sir Ken Robinson hails from Liverpool, England, the same hometown as Sir Paul McCartney. One day as they were comparing notes, Sir Ken discovered that Sir Paul hadn't performed very well in his musical studies. His high school teacher didn't give him good marks and didn't even notice any innate talent. Amazing, right? But it gets even better! George Harrison, lead guitarist for the Beatles, had the same teacher. And he didn't fare any better than McCartney. "Let me get this straight," Ken said to Paul. "This teacher had *half* of the Beatles in his classes and didn't notice anything out of the ordinary?"[31]

Part of the genius of Jesus was His ability to see potential in unlikely places and unlikely people. Where others saw problems, Jesus spied potential.

Remember what the Pharisees said when a prostitute crashed their party? "If this man were a prophet, he would know who is touching him and what kind of woman she is—that she is a sinner."[32] That's half-true. A prophet certainly perceives present-tense realities. Jesus knew exactly who she was, but He also saw who she could become. And He treated her accordingly.

"If you treat an individual as he is, he will remain how he is," said Johann Wolfgang von Goethe. "But if you treat him as if he were what he ought to be and could be, he will become what he ought to be and could be."[33]

The word *prophet* has come to connote doom and gloom, and I'm not suggesting sugarcoating. But, again, a prophetic word strengthens, encourages, and comforts.[34] It's edifying, not insulting. It endows hopefulness, not helplessness. It boldly believes that the best is yet to come.

One Word

Pete Bullette leads Chi Alpha at the University of Virginia, a thriving campus ministry that is influencing hundreds of students. Seventeen years ago Pete did an internship with Chi Alpha in DC and attended National Community Church. One day I sat in on their sermon lab and heard Pete preach. The basement setting wasn't ideal, and neither is preaching to seven people. But God gave me a prophetic word for Pete. I pulled Pete aside afterward and said, "Someday God is going to let you speak to thousands."

Pete found it a little unbelievable at the time, and you better be extra-careful before speaking words like that. The last thing you want to do is set people up for disappointment. Actually, that's the next-to-last thing you want to do. The last thing is not obeying the prompting of the Holy Spirit.

"What you spoke into my life seventeen years ago is now coming to fruition," wrote Pete recently. He speaks to hundreds of students week in and week out, but he had just been invited to speak to a gathering of thousands in Houston, Texas. It was that invitation that prompted his e-mail message. "I don't write this to pat myself on the back," he said. "I write it to close the loop on the prophetic word that has encouraged me for almost two decades."

I'll be the first to confess that I probably miss more opportunities than I seize, but I am always amazed at the power of one prophetic word. And I've been on the receiving end. At a very fragile age and stage in my life, a missionary prayed over me. I'm sure he wouldn't even remember it, but his prayer turned prophetic midstream when he said, "God is going to use you in a great way." I know that sounds awfully generic, but that one sentence has carried me through some tough times.

I'm eternally grateful for the people who pointed out things in me that

I didn't see in myself. No one was better at doing that for people than Jesus, and we're called to follow suit. Again, let's do it in a spirit of humility. And let's exercise emotional intelligence while we're at it. But make no mistake, God wants to speak through you. And it often starts with simply noticing who's next to you.

A Vision for People

I love the story Pastor Erwin McManus shared in a TED Talk about his first TED conference in Tanzania.[35] Erwin is an extreme introvert, so his daughter gave him a few sociability tips: don't hide in a corner, and try not to look too scary. Erwin took her advice and tried to identify the kindest-looking person to have lunch with. He ended up having a very lengthy and interesting conversation with a woman named Jane, but there was something quirky about the conversation. Erwin says, "Have you ever met people who are so passionate about something that no matter what you talk about, they're going to talk about whatever they want to talk about?"

No matter what subject they discussed—from human relationships to geopolitical systems in China—Jane always related it back to chimpanzees. After an hour of this, something dawned on Erwin. He said, "Jane, can I ask you a question? Is your last name Goodall?" Sure enough, Erwin was having lunch with the foremost primatologist in the world, Jane Goodall. And he had no idea for the first hour!

May I make a very blunt observation? Loving your neighbor starts with an awareness of his or her existence. No one is in your life by accident; everyone is there by divine appointment. It's your job not just to notice them but to care for them. And that goes for introverts, extroverts, and everyone in between. The most caring thing you can do is talk to God about them and listen to Him regarding them.

If God gives you a word of encouragement for someone, speak it. You don't have to pronounce, "Thus sayeth the Lord." That might spook them. You might even want to couch it the way Dick Foth does and give them a scale from one to ten. However you approach it, it's your responsibility to love the people God has put in your life, and that means "speaking the truth in love."[36] When you do, one word can make all the difference in the world.

When we hear the word *vision*, we tend to think of some grand objective, such as putting a man on the moon. And that is one type of vision. But the most important kind of vision is a vision for people. And again, Jesus sets the bar.

We don't know much about Mary Magdalene, but we do know that she was possessed by seven demons before Jesus cast them out.[37] Mary had seven problems she couldn't solve. Mary was broken in seven places. Those are the people we tend to give up on, but not God. He won't give up, can't give up! It's not in His nature.

We write off people like Mary, but Jesus writes them in. In fact, Mary became the leading lady in the most important episode in all of Scripture. She was the very first person to witness the resurrection of Jesus Christ and will be forever known as "the apostle to the apostles."[38] Put that on your business card! And that's just like God, isn't it?

We write people off.

Jesus writes people in.

The Ring Master

A few years ago my friend Carlos Whittaker wrote a wonderful book titled *Moment Maker*. I had written *The Circle Maker* a few years before that, so right after his book released, I gave him a fist bump and the customary Super Friends greeting: "Wonder Twins powers activate. Form of the circle maker." He took the cue and said, "Form of the moment maker." Just giving you a glimpse into my second quadrant.

At the beginning of his book, Carlos tells a story about a defining moment in his life. It happened in a preschool classroom in the basement of a church building in Decatur, Georgia. "I was a shy kid," said Carlos, "a Panamanian/Mexican with an Afro parted down the side like Gary Coleman on his best day in a land of bright blond hair, deep blue eyes, and thick southern accents."[39] Carlos was an outlier, and he knew it.

The defining moment happened on the day that parts were handed out for the thirteenth annual Rehoboth Presbyterian Church Preschool Circus. The year before, Carlos had been a lion. His roar had come out more like a meow, and the crowd erupted in laughter. Carlos was scarred with shame, and here he was again at the scene of the crime.

His teacher, Mrs. Stephens, started assigning parts. Mary—dancing bear. Brandon—clown. Jay—muscleman. *Whittaker* is at the end of the alphabet, and when Mrs. Stephens got there, she took off her glasses, smiled a smile that Carlos remembers to this day, and said, "Carlos . . . you are going to be this year's Ring Master."[40]

"That moment, wrapped up in that one sentence, actually changed everything for me. It changed the trajectory of my very future," said Carlos as though it happened yesterday. "She thought *I* could be the Ring Master."[41]

In the eighth grade Carlos would have been content to have been the class treasurer, but he ran for president. Why? Because he was the Ring Master. Carlos has led worship at stadiums filled with tens of thousands of people, and he's been the master of ceremonies at more than a few conferences I've spoken at. Carlos is the master—master of ceremonies! But it traces back to something that a preschool teacher saw in him. She didn't just assign a role in the thirteenth annual Rehoboth Presbyterian Church Preschool Circus; she gave Carlos a new self-image.

What I'm about to say might not sound very exegetical, but I think that is precisely what Paul did for Timothy. Neither Timothy nor Carlos knew where he belonged.[42] I wonder if Timothy would have crawled into his shell and never come out if Paul hadn't spoken that word of exhortation. Timothy would eventually become the Ring Master at the church of Ephesus, but it started with one prophetic word.

Good Grammar

Every language has rules. For example, "*I* before *e* except after *c*." That's especially true of the fifth language. Because it involves at least two personalities, it's twice as complicated as the other languages, and it's more open to misinterpretation.

So here are a few ground rules.

First, *no one is above rebuke.* The minute you think you're beyond temptation, you've fallen into it. Your assignment at the end of this chapter is easy, and it isn't. Give someone permission to speak into your life. Make sure it's someone you trust. And when the person says something you don't want to hear, listen very carefully.

Second, *don't let an arrow of criticism pierce your heart unless it first passes through the filter of Scripture.*[43] And the same goes for compliments. If you live off compliments, you'll probably die by criticisms. Again, we must interpret the language of people through the language of Scripture. If something doesn't add up, throw it out. If it does, repent.

Third, *don't make decisions in a vacuum.* I'm an intrapersonal processor, so I generally process things internally. But as I've already stated, the Bible exhorts us to seek wise counsel. Again, no one shoots the moon by himself. Show me the people you surround yourself with, and I'll show you your future.

Fourth, *listen long and hard before you dish out advice.* The primary reason we don't hear what others have to say is that we're formulating our answers while they're talking. We listen in order to talk instead of listening to listen. One way to make sure we've heard what they said is to practice a counseling technique called restatement. We repeat back what we heard to make sure we got it right.

Fifth, *always encourage before you correct.* That's the pattern in the book of Revelation. God hands down some tough judgments on the seven churches in Revelation but not before He speaks a word of encouragement. Nothing is as disarming as a compliment as long as it's genuine. According to the Losada ratio, we need at least 2.9 instances of positive feedback for every negative feedback.[44] And if you're going to err on one side or the other, err on the side of positivity.

Sixth, *tough conversations get tougher the longer you wait.* I tend to avoid conflict, but I've come to realize that I'm not doing anybody any favors when I do so. Conflict isn't fun, but it helps us grow. Iron doesn't sharpen iron without some sparks flying! Sometimes you have to have what seem to be hurtful conversations with people in order to be helpful, but make sure your motives are right. If you're saying something just to get it off your chest, don't bother. It'll backfire. Genuine relationships are full of grace and truth.

Without grace, relationships have no heart. Without truth, relationships have no head. But when they are full of grace and truth, our relationships ring true. Then and only then will we hear the voice of God through others.

10

THE ARCHER'S PARADOX

The Sixth Language: Promptings

For such a time as this.

—Esther 4:14

Teddy Roosevelt was president of the United States. Henry Ford produced his first Model T.[1] Movies were silent. Women couldn't vote. And a loaf of bread cost five cents, but sliced bread wouldn't be invented for two more decades. Oh, and the Chicago Cubs won the World Series!

The year was 1908.

We would fight two world wars, land a man on the moon, and invent the Internet before the Cubs would win the World Series again in 2016. It had been 108 years, and a baseball is sewn together with 108 stitches. Coincidence? You tell me!

In the top of the tenth inning of game seven, after a gut-wrenching rain delay, Ben Zobrist hit a two-strike double down the third-base line off pitcher Bryan Shaw, driving in the go-ahead run. So many Chicagoans jumped up and down simultaneously that it actually registered on the Richter scale! I'm joking . . . I think. But it did result in the tenth-largest peaceful gathering in human history as reportedly five million Cub fans would "fly the W" a few days later.[2]

That's where I interrupt this fairy-tale ending to the Cubs' curse with a question. How did World Series MVP Ben Zobrist hit that pitch? For that matter how does any batter hit a 2.86-inch diameter baseball that travels 60 feet, 6 inches in 0.43-seconds?[3] It takes one-fifth of a second for the retina to receive incoming messages, and by then the ball is already halfway to home plate.[4] The margin of error between a swing and a hit and a swing and a miss is just 10 milliseconds! That's fifteen times faster than the blink of an eye.[5]

Back to the question. How do you hit a high-inside fastball going a hundred miles per hour or a wicked curveball that can break up to 17.5 inches?[6] The twofold answer is good vision and good timing. Vision without timing takes a strike. Timing without vision swings and misses. It's the unique combination of vision and timing that gets the hit.

We already touched on the importance of vision when we explored the language of dreams. Now it's time to talk about divine timing. Remember the old adage "Timing is everything"? It's as true in life as it is in baseball, and it's especially true when it comes to learning the language of promptings. God is in the business of strategically positioning us in the right place at the right time, but we don't always recognize it as such. He is always right on time, even if it's just in time.

King Solomon said, "There is a time for everything." Then he listed twenty-eight examples.[7] Simply put, you need to know what season you're in. If you don't, you'll get frustrated trying to harvest when it's time to plant or trying to plant when it's time to let the land lie fallow. And the stakes couldn't be any higher. Bad timing can be as calamitous as good timing is fortuitous.

Discerning the voice of God requires an internal clock that perceives His promptings. And it's our reaction time to those promptings that leads to supernatural synchronicities: being in the right place at the right time with the right people. That's precisely what the prophet Isaiah promised:

Whether you turn to the right or to the left, your ears will hear
a voice behind you, saying, "This is the way; walk in it."[8]

Kairos Moments

There are two words for *time* in the New Testament. The first is *chronos,* and it refers to clock time or calendar time. It's where we get our English word *chronology.* Chronos is sequential—past, present, future. And it is linear, moving in only one direction.

According to Greek mythology, Chronos was a short god with muscular legs and winged heels. He moved so fast that once he passed you, he was impossible to catch. To symbolize the transience of time, Chronos had a full head of hair in front but was bald in back. In other words, you can't grasp the present once it's past.[9]

Finally, and most significantly, chronos is a human construct. It's how humans measure time, but God exists outside the space-time dimensions He created. So we have to be very careful not to put Him on our clock, in our box.

The second word for time is *kairos,* and it refers to the opportune time. Chronos is quantitative; it counts minutes. Kairos is qualitative; it captures moments. It's the critical moment or the appointed time—"for such a time as this."[10] It's *carpe diem,* "seize the day."

Kairos is an archery term that denotes an arrow that is fired with sufficient force to penetrate the target.[11] Better yet, it's the archer's paradox. Logic suggests that an arrow be aimed right at a target. But if it's a long distance away, a seasoned archer knows that a vast array of variables will affect the flight path. The arrow must actually be aimed off target in order to hit the target. The ability to evaluate those variables is kairos.

Time management, as in chronos, is important. The psalmist tells us to "number our days."[12] And I believe in Vince Lombardi time: if you aren't fifteen minutes early, you're late! But the apostle Paul took the idea of time management one step further when he told us to redeem the time.[13] It's not the word *chronos;* it's the word *kairos.* And it literally means "making the most of every opportunity."[14]

If you miss the opportunity, it's an opportunity cost. It might even be a sin of omission. If you make the most of an opportunity, it can turn into a defining moment.

I recently spoke at a congressional retreat during a very tense political season. In fact, I had to weave my way through a thousand protestors and a police barricade to get into the hotel where the event was held. My rule of thumb is, if I have an opportunity to preach the gospel, I'll preach to either side of the aisle. That's the example Paul set in his "all things to all people" ministry.[15]

The devotional I shared was during the first session of the day, an optional session, so I was impressed that a few dozen members of both the House and Senate showed up. To be honest, I was a little nervous and had a difficult time figuring out what to say. But as is often the case, the highlight wasn't anything I said. It was a prompting that went past protocol. I felt impressed to ask everyone to kneel for prayer. I wasn't sure how these national leaders would respond to it, but I took the risk that I felt the Holy Spirit was asking me to take. And in a way I never could have predicted or planned, it turned into a holy moment, holy ground. The spiritual and emotional response was visceral. Is kneeling going to solve all our political problems or resolve all our political tensions? No, but it's not a bad place to start.

Chronos time may be measured in minutes, but life is measured in kairos moments. Discerning those moments is part of hearing God's voice. Hearing Him means discerning the holy moments when you need to drop to your knees. It's discerning the critical moments when you need to make a difficult decision. As a parent, it's discerning the teachable moments that can turn into defining moments for your kids.

I hate to admit it, but I miss more kairos moments than I seize. Sometimes I let fear dictate my decisions. I'm afraid of feeling awkward or looking foolish, so I fail to step out in faith. Sometimes I'm too preoccupied with my own problems to discern God's promptings. But listening to those whispers and obeying them can turn an ordinary day into the adventure of a lifetime!

On a Dime

Life turns on a dime, and the dime is the decisions that change the trajectory of our lives forever. Some of them are well thought out, while others happen on a whim. Either way, it would be terrifying if it weren't for God's ordering our footsteps, wouldn't it?

At the beginning of my junior year at Central Bible College, there was a special service in which local pastors were invited to chapel. It was the beginning of a new year, and the school wanted to get us plugged into a local church. There must have been fifty pastors packed into the choir loft, and I recognized a few of the faces because they had preached in chapel or pastored one of the larger churches in town.

I knew that most of the students would land at whatever church was the "it" church that semester. And I was thinking about doing the same thing. I was playing basketball along with taking a full load of classes, so I was tempted to attend a church with a great preacher where I could just sit back and relax.

That's when I felt a strange prompting. I'd never felt a leading quite like it before, but I knew exactly which pastor I was supposed to talk to. I can't explain how or why; I just knew. Right after chapel I made a beeline to Pastor Robert Smiley, and I think I was the only one who did. I didn't know him, but he knew me because he followed our basketball team.

I would spend two years of college not just attending West Grand Assembly of God but serving in a wide variety of ways. That church doesn't exist anymore, and it barely existed then. On a good Sunday, a dozen people would show up. And that almost packed the place, as there were only seven pews! But I'm forever indebted to Pastor Smiley, who let me cut my teeth preaching. He even let me lead worship on occasion and do "special" music once!

I'm absolutely convinced that I wouldn't have been ready to plant a church in my twenties if it hadn't been for Pastor Smiley. He's part of my cloud of witnesses. And it all started with a prompting.

Time Sensitive

Truth isn't relative, but time is. Parents of toddlers, you know this. To two-year-olds, next week might as well be next year, and next year might as well be never. Why? Because one year represents 50 percent of their lives. If you're fifty, a year represents 2 percent. To children, one day can feel twenty-five times longer than it does to their parents, and it might be even more pronounced for the children of God.

With God, "a thousand years are like a day"![16]

With us, a day can feel like a thousand years!

Those of us who were born after Neil Armstrong took "one small step for man" operate on a different time line than our parents. We microwave our food, Google our questions, real-time our news, and Facebook our friends.

Everything happens at the speed of light. But in God's kingdom, things happen at the speed of a seed planted in the ground that has to take root before it can bear fruit. I love millennials, and that's primarily who I pastor. I love their passion for justice, their desire to make a difference, and their pragmatic idealism. I'm also concerned about what I perceive to be a lack of patience. I'm guilty of it too. We want what our parents have in half the time with half the effort. But I can almost guarantee that our hopes and dreams will take longer than our original estimates.

Here's the point: we give up too easily, too quickly. We often get ahead of God instead of keeping in step with the Spirit, or we fall behind out of frustration. It's not easy discerning His timing, and it's even harder trusting it, especially when it feels as though God is a day late and a dollar short. But if you're questioning His timing, perhaps it's your watch that needs to be adjusted. You get in time with Him by getting in tune with His whisper.

For David's Sake

Versions of this three-word phrase—"For David's sake"—pop up in multiple places in the Old Testament.[17] It's a testament to God's faithfulness even when we're faithless.

In 853 BC, a king named Jehoram assumed the throne. He was the fifth king of the southern kingdom, and he did what was evil in the eyes of the Lord. Jehoram actually killed his brothers to secure the throne. You would expect God to execute judgment in the next verse, wouldn't you? Not so fast.

Nevertheless, *for the sake of his servant David,* the LORD was not willing to destroy Judah.[18]

This is 117 years after David's death! David is long gone, but God hasn't forgotten the promise He made. God has a good memory. He doesn't forget His people, and He doesn't forget His promises. The only thing He forgets is the sin He forgives.

Can I suggest that God has done some things in your life for the sake of someone else?

I know He has for me. I had a praying grandfather in Elmer Johnson. At night he would take off his hearing aid, kneel next to his bed, and pray. He couldn't hear himself, but everyone else in the house could. Those are some of my earliest memories. My grandfather died when I was six, but his prayers did not. There have been distinct moments in my life when I've received a blessing I know I didn't deserve, and the Holy Spirit has whispered these words: *Mark, the prayers of your grandfather are being answered in your life right now.* That will give you goose bumps! God did it "for Elmer's sake."

We're the beneficiaries of prayers we know nothing about. God was working long before we arrived on the scene, and He's using us to set up the next generation.

We tend to think right here, right now.

God is thinking nations and generations.

We have no idea how our lives are going to alter the course of history downstream, but there is a divine domino effect for every decision we make. Don't underestimate the potential impact of obeying God's prompts. Those are the whispers that will echo for all eternity!

Unanswered Prayers

During the early days of our church planting, our church office was a spare bedroom in our home. When our daughter, Summer, was born, it doubled as church office by day and bedroom by night. That got really old really fast, so we started looking for office space. I found two row houses on Capitol Hill that were absolutely perfect, and I let God know that. But both doors closed in dramatic fashion. In both instances another party beat us to the punch and put contracts on those properties right before we did. Not only did God not answer our prayers, but it felt as if He was opposing our efforts. It was so confusing and frustrating that I almost gave up the hunt.

A few weeks later I was walking by 205 F Street when I felt a very strange prompting. It was as though the Holy Spirit jogged my memory and surfaced a name. I had met the owner of that row house a year before, but I wasn't sure the name that had surfaced out of my subconscious was his name. This was pre-Google, so I actually had to look up the name in something called the white pages, and there were eight listings of that name. There wasn't even a For Sale sign in front of the house. Why would I call him? And what would I say? But I obeyed that prompting by dialing a phone number I wasn't sure was his.

When someone answered the phone, I quickly introduced myself. But the person on the other end of the line wouldn't let me finish my sentence. "I was just thinking about you," he said. "I'm considering selling 205 F Street, and I wanted to know if you would like to buy it before I put it on the market."

That's *kairos*!

That row house became our first office. But even more significant than its function was its location, because 205 F Street is next to 201 F Street, an old crack house that would become Ebenezers Coffeehouse! If God had answered our original prayers for the two row homes that were "absolutely perfect," we wouldn't have been in the position to buy and build our coffeehouse. So praise God for unanswered prayers!

Our heavenly Father is far too wise to always give us what we want when we want it. He loves us too much to do that. Don't settle for what's expedient. Don't settle for second best. Hold out for the best that God can give. Then hold on.

Supernatural Insomnia

A great biblical example of divine timing and prompting may be a case of supernatural insomnia. In the book of Esther, the Jewish people were on the brink of genocide because of a plot hatched by an evil man named Haman. His archenemy was Mordecai, Queen Esther's cousin. Haman hated Mordecai so much that he erected a seventy-five-foot pole on which to impale him! But on the eve of Mordecai's execution, God showed up and showed off.

> That night the king could not sleep; so he ordered the book of the
> chronicles, the record of his reign, to be brought in and read to him.
> It was found recorded there that Mordecai had exposed Bigthana
> and Teresh, two of the king's officers who guarded the doorway, who
> had conspired to assassinate King Xerxes.[19]

You can read the rest of the story in the book of Esther, but God flipped the script in one fell swoop. Mordecai, riding the king's horse and wearing the king's robe, was given a ticker-tape parade through the streets of Susa, and Haman was impaled on the gallows he built!

A few key observations.

First, *God doesn't always reward good deeds on the spot.* Have you ever done something that seemingly went unnoticed? It's frustrating at the time, but I've learned to trust God's time line. He doesn't always reward us right then or right there. But I promise you this: He'll reward your faithfulness somehow, someway, sometime. Mordecai had saved the life of King Xerxes by foiling an assassination plot, but he must have felt as though his good deed had been forgotten. Yet God was making sure it was remembered and rewarded at just the right time, just in time.

Second, *insomnia is sometimes a sign that God wants to speak to us.* When I wake up at a strange hour for a strange reason, I take it as a prompting to pray. Sure, it's sometimes caused by poor dietary choices the night before, but not always. Why not pray until you fall back asleep? It beats counting sheep.

Third, *God can accomplish more in one day than you can accomplish in a lifetime.*

Now let's have a little fun with this story. What are the chances that King Xerxes would get a case of insomnia on the eve of Mordecai's execution? For the sake of simplicity, let's call it 1 in 365. As the ruling monarch, King Xerxes probably had the biggest library in Persia. There is no way to know its exact contents, but I wouldn't be surprised if it was on par with the Royal Library of Ashurbanipal. The British Museum puts the number of Ashurbanipal's holdings at 30,943 scrolls and tablets.[20] If we use that as a benchmark, the chances of King Xerxes choosing the book of the chronicles was 1 in 30,943.

Finally, we have no idea how big the book of the king's reign was, but I bet it was closer to an encyclopedia than a comic book. At the end of every day that Congress is in session, the proceedings are printed in the *Congressional Record.* The record includes the opening prayer and Pledge of Allegiance, along with petitions, nominations, text amendments, and joint resolutions. The record of the first day of the 115th Congress was 101 pages long.[21] Of course it included the election of the Speaker of the House of Representatives, so it might be a little above average. And I'm sure the Persians weren't as copious as we are. But Xerxes reigned for twenty-one years. My point? It was a big book! We'll keep it conservative and put the odds of the book being opened to that very page, that very paragraph about Mordecai as 1 in 1,000.

When we multiply those numbers, the odds of Xerxes landing on the page profiling Mordecai's good deed is 1 in 11,294,195,000. That's when you know that God is part of the equation!

Discerning the difference between coincidence and providence cannot be reduced to a mathematical formula, but God loves pulling off the impossible against all odds. He also loves using the least qualified candidate to accomplish His plans and purposes.

Crazy Promptings

On February 24, 1958, *Life* magazine published a feature article titled "Mass Murder Trial of a Teen-Age Gang." It pictured seven gang members accused of murdering Michael Farmer, a fifteen-year-old boy disabled by polio. The trial arrested the nation's attention, not unlike the O. J. Simpson trial almost four decades later. But it totally wrecked a Pennsylvania pastor named David Wilkerson. One of the boy's faces—the meanest of the seven—was seared in his memory. Others read the article, but Wilkerson wept over it without knowing why.

Wilkerson would go on to start a worldwide ministry called Teen Challenge, write a *New York Times* bestselling book titled *The Cross and the Switchblade,* and start Times Square Church. But it all started with one prompting: a magazine article. Like Paul reacting to the vision of a man in Macedonia calling for help, Wilkerson could not ignore what he perceived to be a whisper from God. Sitting in his study late on a Sunday night in February 1958, he discerned the voice of God: "Go to New York and help those boys."[22]

Moving from rural Pennsylvania to minister to the gangs of New York City was a crazy prompting but not any crazier than some of the promptings recorded in Scripture. It was a crazy prompting that led a cupbearer in Babylon to rebuild the wall of Jerusalem. It was a crazy prompting that led Philip to intersect with an Ethiopian eunuch in the middle of nowhere. It was a crazy prompting that led Ananias to pray for a terrorist named Saul. And it was a crazy prompting that led to a divine appointment between a Jewish apostle named Peter and an Italian soldier named Cornelius.[23]

Prior to reading that article in *Life,* David Wilkerson had gone on a mission trip to Argentina. That trip produced a "restlessness"[24] in his spirit. It's difficult to define the feeling, but it's a sixth sense that God is getting you ready for something else, someplace else. "Sometimes you have to go halfway around the world," noted his son Gary, "to realize you're not called there."[25] That mission trip produced not only a restlessness but an openness to go anywhere, to do anything. And in my experience that's what mission trips do. When you get out of your comfort zone, you hear God's voice more clearly. It's often a door that leads to a door. Or maybe I should say, a prompting that leads to a prompting.

Effective Frequency

Let me zoom out and make an important observation. Learning to discern God's promptings takes practice. Remember, it's like learning a new language. You don't always pick up on the nuances at first. But if you give it some time, you'll get better at hearing those subtle whispers. And the good news is that God is patient. It's not three strikes and you're out in God's kingdom. It's more like "seventy times seven" second chances![26]

There is a phenomenon in advertising known as effective frequency, which refers to the number of times you have to hear a message before you'll respond to it. The rule of seven was the rule of thumb for a long time, but the magic number seems to be climbing. Maybe because there are so many voices vying for our attention.

"Just do it."

"Plop, plop, fizz, fizz, oh what a relief it is."

"Breakfast of champions."

I don't need to tell you who ran those ads, do I? You know it was Nike, Alka-Seltzer, and Wheaties. Did you know that those ad campaigns ran twenty-six, forty-three, and eighty-seven years respectively?[27] They are brilliant examples of effective frequency, and it seems to me that God advertises His plans and purposes in much the same way. He patiently prompts us over and over and over again. And He often does it by using various languages.

Have you noticed the different ways in which God got someone's attention in Scripture? And the number of times it took? It's a study in effective frequency. For Samuel, the effective frequency was four late-night whispers. For Peter, the effective frequency was an early-morning rooster crowing twice. For Saul, the effective frequency was a vision and a voice at midday.[28]

If you're anything like me, it takes God a few times to get your full attention. And that's why He speaks in stereo. In other words, He whispers in more than one language. It's His way of making doubly or triply sure that we're picking up what He's throwing down. And for those of us who are a little slow on the uptake, God is gracious enough to give two or three or four confirmations. The apostle Paul is Exhibit A, and Ananias is the key witness.

> Go to the house of Judas on Straight Street and ask for a man
> from Tarsus named Saul, for he is praying. In a vision he has seen
> a man named Ananias come and place his hands on him to restore
> his sight.[29]

Wouldn't you think that knocking Saul off his horse on the road to Damascus would have been enough of a sign to turn him into Paul? But Saul's effective frequency required a little more than that. First, God spoke in an audible voice from heaven. Second, He spoke through a double vision: Saul had a vision of Ananias while Ananias had a vision of Saul. Third, God spoke to Ananias with very detailed directions to find Saul on Straight Street. And fourth, He spoke by miraculously healing Paul's eyesight. That's stereo surround sound. That's effective frequency. That was God making quadruply sure Saul heard His voice.

Status-Quo Bias

The Holy Spirit wears lots of hats in Scripture. He hovers, gifts, convicts, reveals, and reminds. But when He wants to get us out of our routines, He often stirs our spirits.

> The LORD stirred up the spirit of Zerubbabel.[30]

The stirring of the Holy Spirit can be a feeling of restlessness, as David Wilkerson experienced. Sometimes it starts out as a God-ordained desire that becomes fire in our bones. Sometimes it's an idea that hits critical mass. And sometimes God rocks the boat—or capsizes it.

You can call it a ping, a poke, a nudge, or an impression. I call it a prompting, and I liken it to the Holy Spirit's elbow right in our ribs! The Spirit often stirs us in the same way that we're called to spur one another toward good deeds. It's the motivation to stop, to start, or to change.

This is a strange bit of personal trivia, but I always set my alarm to an even number. I'm not sure why I do this, but I know I'm not alone. Every time I confess this idiosyncrasy, "even" people come out of the closet. Some "odd" people do too! Either way, we're creatures of habit. Our natural tendency is to do what we've been doing, think what we've been thinking, and say what we've been saying.

My affinity for even numbers when it comes to alarm clocks is an example of a phenomenon called the status-quo bias. The term was first employed by two psychologists, William Samuelson and Richard Zeckhauser, in the *Journal of Risk and Uncertainty* nearly three decades ago.[31] Simply put, it's the tendency to keep doing what you've been doing without giving it much thought.

Have you ever been offered a free one-year subscription to a magazine? Magazines are so generous, right? Wrong! Magazine companies and cell phone companies and cable television companies and credit card companies all understand the status-quo bias. After the introductory offer is over, you'll forget to cancel. And even if you don't forget, you're too lazy to make a phone call to cancel the product or service. It's human nature to keep doing what you've been doing, and here's the problem: if you keep doing what you've always done, you'll keep getting what you've always gotten. To expect otherwise is the definition of insanity.

The status-quo bias is a major impediment to spiritual growth. And if we aren't careful, it'll keep us from discerning God's promptings.

In computer science, default settings are automatically assigned to software applications, computer programs, and smartphones. Those out-of-the-box settings are called presets, and their purpose is to establish a protocol to optimize performance.

In much the same way, we all have default settings that dictate a lot of what we do. From the way we wake up, to the way we eat, to the way we interact with others, so many dimensions of our lives become patterned. A handful of default settings dictate our thoughts and actions. And the good news is this: a small change in a preset can have a huge change in outcome.

A few years ago I was trying to drop a few pounds, but I was having the hardest time shedding the weight. I was venting to a friend of mine while drinking a Venti Caramel Macchiato at Starbucks one night when he looked down at my drink and said, "You know you're sabotaging yourself, right?" A Venti Caramel Macchiato is 250 calories, and that was my second one of the day! So what did I do? I did the only thing I could do if I wanted to lose weight: I changed my default drink.

Heeding a little prompting today can have a huge net effect tomorrow.

The Nudge Unit

In 2010 the British government tasked a seven-person team with improving government programs based upon behavioral science. Formally called the Behavioural Insights Team, it became known as the Nudge Unit. The team was given a modest budget, and a sunset clause ensured that their experiment could be halted if they didn't see any results.

The team leader, David Halpern, gave his first official report twenty months into David Cameron's administration as prime minister. The cabinet secretaries were a little cynical, but Halpern won them over with four slides. The first slide showed that a very small edit in language increased the collection of taxes by tens of millions of pounds. The second slide noted that the best way to get people to insulate their attics was to offer an "attic clearance service." The third slide revealed that including the image of a car captured by a roadside camera significantly increased the payment of traffic violations. And the fourth slide showed that sending texts to perpetrators who had overdue fines doubled the response rate.[32]

The name Nudge Unit was a tip of the cap to authors Richard Thaler and Cass Sunstein, who coined the concept with their bestselling book *Nudge*. A nudge is a means of encouraging and guiding behavior without mandating or instructing it. And it's evidence that small changes in input can make dramatic differences in outcome.

The classic example is the men's restroom at Schiphol Airport in Amsterdam. The restroom designer, Aad Kieboom, etched the image of a black housefly into each urinal, which reduced spillage by 80 percent. According to Kieboom, "If a man sees a fly, he aims at it."[33]

Another fun example is on Chicago's Lake Shore Drive. When drivers fail to observe the speed limit of twenty-five miles per hour, the series of S curves is quite dangerous. So what did the city of Chicago do? They painted a series of white stripes progressively closer and closer together before the curve, giving the sensation that one is actually speeding up. The natural reaction? To slow down.[34]

"When we drive on this familiar stretch of road," noted Thaler and Sunstein, "we find that those lines are speaking to us, gently urging us to touch the brake before the apex of the curve. We have been nudged."[35]

In my experience God gently nudges us in much the same way. A fleeting thought here, a surge of adrenaline there. Or, as for David Wilkerson, a little restlessness here or a lot of anguish there. Thaler and Sunstein have a name for those who design nudges: choice architects.[36] And no one is better at it than the Holy Spirit.

When God prompts you to pray, pray.

When God prompts you to serve, serve.

When God prompts you to give, give.

God is setting you up, but you have to obey the prompting. And your obedience—whether it's praying, serving, or giving—might just be somebody else's miracle.

Seth Bolt makes a living by creating music and performing in cities all over the world with the band Needtobreathe. That's his passion and his calling. What many people don't know, however, is that when Seth isn't working for the band, he and his wife, Tori, have a side project they are passionate about as well. In 2015 Seth and his father built a luxury tree house in upstate South Carolina. It was there that Seth and Tori were married and celebrated their honeymoon, and since then the tree house has been a blessing to guests who have come from around the world to stay and sway in its branches.

Not long after their wedding, Seth and Tori dreamed of building tree houses of their own in Charleston, South Carolina. They not only wanted a place to retreat when they are off the road but a place where others could come to reconnect with God. After reading *The Circle Maker,* Seth and Tori started circling a thirty-acre property near Charleston on Wadmalaw Island. They absolutely fell in love with the property and its moss-covered oaks, but that's when reality hit. The price tag was outside their budget, way outside their budget. They could afford only half the land, but a bidding war had produced full-price offers for the entire property. That's when Seth and Tori felt prompted to take a step of faith.

Before I share the rest of the story, let me share a few convictions. Faith doesn't ignore reality, including financial reality. Faith counts the cost— actual costs and opportunity costs. But when things don't add up, faith doesn't always walk away in defeat. Faith knows that God can make up the difference, no matter how big a difference it is. Why? Because God owns the cattle on a thousand hills! And when God gives the vision, He makes provision.

For more than a year, Seth and Tori searched for their piece of promised land, and they asked God to give them a sign. Their fleece? They prayed that God would send a bald eagle. On the day they had to make one of the most difficult decisions of their lives—make an offer or walk away—an eagle landed on one of those mossy oaks about fifty feet from them. Seth and Tori knew it wasn't mere coincidence. It was providence. By faith they signed the contract. And when they finished signing, the bald eagle flew away. Can you say divine timing? But that's not nearly as amazing as what happened the very next day.

What Seth and Tori didn't know when they took that step of faith is they weren't the only ones circling the thirty acres in prayer. Another couple was circling the same property at the same time, but they weren't circling it to buy it. They were simply circling it for God's plans, God's purposes. When this couple, whom Seth and Tori had met only once and briefly, discovered the Bolts' God-given dream for the property, this couple offered to give them the difference! Notice the word *give*, not *lend*. Who does that? Who gives virtual strangers a significant chunk of change to make their dream come true? I'll tell you who—someone who listens to and obeys the still small voice of God.

In Tori's words, "You can't make this stuff up! God answers prayer!"

Sixty Seconds Flat

I've shared my bravest prayer and a few unanswered prayers. Let me also share what might be the fastest answer to prayer ever! When we first moved to Washington, I directed an inner-city parachurch ministry called the Urban Bible Training Center. Lora and I were living paycheck to paycheck, or maybe I should say offering to offering since I was an itinerant preacher. And the ministry wasn't even close to being self-supporting when I felt a prompting to give to another parachurch ministry in the city. The prompting didn't make sense financially. How can you give what you don't have? It took as much faith as I had to write a $350 check, and I had to shut down my logical left brain long enough to drop the check in the mailbox outside the post office.

After dropping it off, I went inside to retrieve my mail from our post office box. Inside the box was a letter from the Mustard Seed Foundation with a check for $10,000. That's a 2,857 percent return in sixty seconds flat.

I don't believe in "name it, claim it."

I don't believe you can outgive God either.

When sixty seconds is all that separates giving and receiving, it's hard to miss the cause and effect. It was a Luke 6:38 moment: "Give, and it will be given to you. A good measure, pressed down, shaken together and running over, will be poured into your lap. For with the measure you use, it will be measured to you."

God is not a slot machine. And the reward we're looking for is eternal, not material. But He cannot be outgiven. If you give for the wrong reasons, it doesn't count in His kingdom. But if you give for the right reasons, it's game on! The mailbox at 45 L Street NW is one of my burning bushes. God whispered, loud and clear!

The Power of a Single Prompting

Now let me double back to David Wilkerson. After obeying the prompting to move to New York City, Wilkerson led the head of the infamous Mau Maus gang, Nicky Cruz, to Christ. John Sherrill, an editor at *Guideposts*, turned that testimony into the first multipart story that magazine had ever published. And that *Guideposts* story eventually became *The Cross and the Switchblade*, a *New York Times* bestseller that sold more than fifteen million copies.

As an author, I love the way this book deal went down, and it's a testament to the power of a single prompting. Instead of seeking a Christian publisher, David Wilkerson and John Sherrill approached Bernard Geis, one of the pioneers of sensational publishing in the 1960s. Geis was on the cusp of releasing Helen Gurley Brown's *Sex and the Single Girl,* a book that would sell two million copies in its first three weeks![37] He was a master of staging stunts and creating controversy to sell copies, so what would a publisher like that want with a preacher like David Wilkerson?

Landing a contract was a long shot, to say the least. So Wilkerson told Sherrill that he wanted to put a fleece before the Lord. Sherrill didn't even know what a fleece was. Wilkerson did exactly what I did when we explored the language of doors. He explained the way Gideon discerned the will of God by giving Him very specific and practical conditions by which to reveal His will.

Wilkerson laid down two fleeces in prayer before the Lord. The first fleece was that Geis, a very busy executive, would be able to meet with them that same day—a Friday. If you've ever submitted a book proposal, you know that pub boards don't work that way. It's usually a much longer process. The second fleece was that Geis would offer them a $5,000 advance on the spot. "That doesn't sound like much," said Sherrill in retrospect, "but back then you could buy a house with it."[38]

The first condition was met when Geis offered them ten minutes that afternoon, but he seemed nonplussed by their pitch. What got his attention? He genuinely admired Wilkerson's guts in risking his life to reach the gangs of New York, and although Geis was irreligious, he couldn't believe that gang members and heroin addicts were finding religion. "Write up a proposal," said Geis. "If it's a go, I'll give you five thousand dollars."[39]

But the story doesn't end there.

Goose Bumps

In 1968 a Hollywood actor and singer named Pat Boone read the book that Bernard Geis published. In Boone's words, "I got goose bumps."[40] I've already outlined what I call the Goose-Bump Test, but let me take it one step further. Physiologically, goose bumps are an involuntary reaction to a strong emotion. In this instance I believe they were the initial physical evidence of a spiritual stirring. That feeling is a prompting. And it led to a film version of *The Cross and the Switchblade*, in which Pat Boone played the role of David Wilkerson. The Hollywood Foreign Press Association didn't give the movie a Golden Globe, but it ranks as one of the most watched films in the world, viewed by fifty million people in 150 countries.[41] And it started with goose bumps.

I realize that goose bumps might not be a litmus test for intellectual types, and I don't recommend making life-altering decisions in an emotionally heightened state. But don't discount intuition either. In fact, pay close attention to the things that make your hair stand on end.

Linda Kaplan Thaler is the advertising guru responsible for the little jingle "I don't wanna grow up, I'm a Toys R Us kid." She also came up with "Kodak moments."[42] How does Linda discern good ideas from duds? Without a hint of apology, she said, "Chills are how I ran the Kodak business."[43]

I would highly recommend test marketing, strategizing, and planning.

But some of the best ideas in business start out as goose bumps. And that's true of the Father's business as well. Goose bumps aren't one of the seven love languages I outline in this book, but they're a subdialect. Don't ignore those things that give you chills. Perhaps you're hearing from the same Holy Spirit who "warmed" the heart of John Wesley.

It's impossible to calculate the full impact of anyone's life because our influence outlives us. That's true of a film, a book, or an organization as well. But I think it's fair to say that David Wilkerson's influence exceeded his wildest imagination. And like so many miracles, it started as a whisper. If he had ignored the prompting that came through that 1958 *Life* article, how many subsidiary stories would have gone untold? The same goes for Pat Boone's prompting that came via those goose bumps.

At the end of our lives, we'll all have our fair share of regrets because of the mistakes we've made. But I bet we'll regret even more the opportunities we missed. That's how and why and when we fall short of God's glory. So how do we make sure we don't miss those God-ordained opportunities? We have to turn up the volume on the still small voice of God and make sure He's the loudest voice in our lives.

11

JOYSTICK

The Seventh Language: Pain

In the towns of Judah and the streets of Jerusalem that are deserted, inhabited by neither people nor animals, there will be heard once more the sounds of joy and gladness.

—JEREMIAH 33:10–11

Martin Pistorius was a happy, healthy little boy. But when he was twelve, a mysterious illness left him comatose for three years. When he finally woke up, he was unable to move, unable to speak. Locked-in syndrome paralyzes all the voluntary muscles in the body with one curious exception: vertical eye movement. Martin was reduced to a persistent vegetative state. Specialists told his parents that he had zero intelligence, zero awareness. The specialists were wrong, but Martin had no way of proving it. He had no capacity to communicate his thoughts or feelings with the outside world; he was a prisoner trapped inside his own body.

Martin was dropped off at a medical care center day after day, week after week, month after month for thirteen and a half years. When he was force-fed scalding-hot food, he couldn't voice how much it hurt. When he needed assistance, he couldn't even cry like a baby. And because the specialists thought his intelligence level was that of a toddler, Martin was placed in front of a television tuned to *Barney & Friends* and *Teletubbies.*

A silent witness to the world around him, Martin felt totally alone, totally powerless. Well, almost. "I was completely entombed," says Martin in his memoir, *Ghost Boy*. "The only person who knew there was a boy within the useless shell was God, and I had no idea why I felt His presence so strongly. He was with me as my mind knitted itself back together. He was as present to me as air, as constant as breathing."[1]

Everyone, even his mother and father, acted as if Martin didn't exist. No one thought he was there—no one except a nurse named Virna, who believed that Martin was more aware than anyone realized. Virna had seen a television program about a new technology that enabled stroke victims who couldn't speak to communicate with the help of an electronic device. Then she whispered words of hope: "Do you think you could do something like that, Martin? I'm sure you could."[2] Because of Virna's persistence, Martin was taken to the Centre for Augmentative and Alternative Communication at the University of Pretoria, South Africa. Using infrared sensors that tracked eye movement, a doctor asked Martin to identify pictures on the screen: first a ball, then a dog, then a television. Martin used the one thing he could control—eye movement—to identify each and every object.

More than thirteen years after contracting the illness that trapped him inside his body, Martin learned to communicate with a computerized voice using a joystick. Two years later he got his first job. He went to college. He started his own company. He got married. He wrote a book. And he did it all with a joystick.

I know some of you reading this book feel a lot like Martin: so discouraged, so scared, so frustrated, so misunderstood. Even in a crowd you feel lonely. You have your good days, but they're short lived. And you never know when depression is going to come knocking.

You need to know that you're not alone.

There isn't one of us who doesn't wrestle with shameful secrets, debilitating fears, and bitter memories. If statistics hold true, 6.7 percent of us deal with depression, 8.7 percent have some sort of phobia, and 18 percent have an anxiety disorder.[3] Those emotional challenges are real, but so is hope.

Rock Bottom

The Bible is a book about real people with real problems who experienced real pain. It starts in the Garden of Eden with one sinful decision. The initial consequences were pain in childbirth and painful toil to produce food.[4] But the net effect is pain across the board: physical, emotional, and spiritual. The good news is that heaven is a pain-free zone.[5] But between here and there, pain is guaranteed.

The oldest book of the Bible is Job, and Job's life is the epitome of pain and suffering. Job lost his family to a catastrophe. He lost his wealth and his health. Worst of all, he lost hope. He was a defeated man and eventually asked God to end his life. But even in the most calamitous circumstances, he had a very thin thread of joy: "I would still have this consolation—my joy in unrelenting pain—that I had not denied the words of the Holy One."[6]

The New American Standard Bible says, "I rejoice in unsparing pain."

The Holman Christian Standard Bible says, "I would leap for joy in unrelenting pain."

The English Standard Version says, "I would even exult in pain unsparing."

This Hebrew word for "joy" appears only once in Scripture—it's rare joy, extreme joy. It's a joy that doesn't deny reality, but it does defy it. It's triumphant elation in the face of staggering loss. The most literal translation is this: "to leap like a horse so stones spark."[7] It's not just jumping for joy; it's dancing on disappointment.

Somehow Job took a small measure of pleasure despite the pain. Would he have changed the circumstances if he could have? In a heartbeat. But Job found joy in one simple fact: he didn't deny the words of the Holy One.

In the midst of tough times, we may feel as if the Almighty has turned His back on us. So what do we usually want to do? We tend to turn our back on Him. But that's when we need to lean in and lean on Him. And that's what Job did. He didn't cut God off; he didn't stop listening.

Can I challenge you to do the same?

Perhaps God is saying something that can't be heard any other way.

This is the toughest chapter for me to write, and it's probably the toughest one to read. Pain isn't pleasant. But C. S. Lewis was spot-on: "God whispers to us in our pleasures . . . but shouts in our pain."[8]

Please hear me. Every pleasure known to man is a gift from God.

Sex? God's idea.

Food? God's idea.

Recreation? God's idea.

Those pleasures turn into pain when we misuse and abuse them, but make no mistake, every pleasure in its purest form is a gift from God. Yes, we can turn them into sinful pursuits when we try to meet legitimate needs in illegitimate ways. But pleasure is a gift from God nonetheless. He whispers through those pleasures, and we should give thanks for them. But we better pay close attention to pain too.

The Gift of Pain

Before we go any further, dare I mention that pain can be a gift? Without pain we would repeatedly reinjure ourselves in the same ways. Without pain we would simply maintain the status quo. Without pain we would ignore problems that can kill us.

In fact, pain saved my life on July 23, 2000. I woke up that Sunday morning with intense pain in my abdomen, but I ignored it. I tried to preach a sermon that Sunday, but it became the only sermon I didn't finish. Five minutes into it I was doubled over in pain. I ended up in the emergency room at Washington Hospital Center, where an MRI revealed ruptured intestines. I was immediately wheeled into surgery, where I could have and perhaps should have died. And I certainly would have died if it weren't for the intense pain I could not ignore.

I was on a respirator for two days, fighting for my life. I lost twenty-five pounds in seven days. Trust me, there are better ways to lose weight! And the net result is a foot-long scar that bisects my abdomen from top to bottom. Sometimes the greatest joy follows the worst pain, as mothers of newborns can attest. Few people inflict more pain on themselves than athletes, but the pain is forgotten in the thrill of victory.

Would I want to experience another brush with death like that? Not on my life! But I wouldn't trade it for anything in the world. I don't take a single day for granted. And the presence of God during those difficult days was as real as anything I've ever felt. It's a presence that is felt and a voice that is heard most clearly during pain.

Remember Joseph in the Old Testament? He had zero emotional intelligence as a teenager, which isn't entirely uncommon. But thirteen years of suffering earned him a graduate degree in empathy. And it was one act of empathy—noticing a dejected look on the face of a fellow prisoner—that eventually led to saving two nations.

Pain can be a professor of theology.

Pain can be a marriage counselor.

Pain can be a life coach.

Nothing gets our full attention like pain. It breaks down false idols and purifies false motives. It reveals where we need to heal, where we need to grow. It refocuses priorities like nothing else. And pain is part and parcel of God's sanctification process in our lives.

Many lead actors and actresses in Scripture endured dark nights of the soul. Job lost everything. Sarah wrestled with infertility. Moses was a fugitive for forty years. David had a father-in-law who tried to kill him. Mary Magdalene was demon possessed. Peter struggled with self-doubt after he denied even knowing Jesus. And Paul had memories of murder seared into his soul. They also had one thing in common: they heard God's whisper in their darkest hours. And they all came out the other side by His grace.

My prayer for you isn't that you'd be pain-free; it's that you'd learn to discern God's loving voice in the midst of the pain. Is there a lesson He is trying to teach you? Is there some part of your character that can't be cultivated any other way?

I'm certainly not suggesting that all pain is caused by God. Pain is a result of the curse, and it's most often a symptom of sin. But sometimes it's a gift from God. It's the language that can't be ignored. You can leave the Bible on your bedside table untouched. You can ignore desires, dreams, doors, promptings, and people. But you can't ignore pain, can you?

If you will stick with me through the next few pages, I promise that the following statement will make more sense: pain can be a gift from God that He uses for His glory and our good. He uses it to get us out of addictive behaviors. He uses it to get us out of adverse situations. He uses it to get us out of abusive relationships. Take note and get out.

The miracle that Jesus repeated perhaps more than any other was the healing of lepers. Have you ever stopped to consider what that miracle accomplished? Among other things, He was restoring their sense of touch. One curse of leprosy is the loss of feeling. Lepers can't feel pain or pleasure. They become numb to the physical world around them, and that's a dangerous way to live. So Jesus gave them the gift of touch again, a gift that includes both pleasure and pain.

Growing Pains

The expression "No pain, no gain" is older than you might imagine. It didn't originate with Jane Fonda's workout videos in the 1980s. It dates back to a second-century Jewish rabbi who said, "According to the pain is the gain."[9]

Let's be honest. Most of us prefer this philosophy: no pain, no pain. We opt for the path of least resistance, but that doesn't get us where God wants us to go. I'm certainly not suggesting that we need to seek out pain. Pain will find us soon enough. But when pain comes, we shouldn't try to go around it. Instead, we need to go through it and learn to discern what God is saying through pain, through grief, and through suffering.

If it serves a higher purpose, pain can actually produce a measure of pleasure. When God answered my bravest prayer and healed my asthma, I decided to celebrate and validate that healing miracle by training for my first marathon. The eighteen-week training plan is one of the hardest things I've ever done. I basically inflict more and more pain on myself by running longer and longer distances. But when I cross the finish line of the Chicago Marathon, the pain will be in the past. The memory of that accomplishment, however, will last forever.

When I work out, one of my soundtracks is the training montage from *Rocky IV.* It helps me get a few extra reps, a few extra steps. I've seen the movie so many times that I can picture Rocky Balboa running up a snow-covered mountain. Rocky saws wood, splits logs. He does dogsled bear crawls and walking lunges with a wooden beam through waist-deep snow. He does Roman chair sit-ups in an old barn, core work with an ox yoke, and the shoulder press with a horse carriage. Basically the same as your workout routine, right? Or not. But how else are you going to beat Ivan Drago?

Do you remember the two-word mantra repeated by Rocky's trainer, Duke, over and over again? I sometimes hear it in my head when I hit the wall during a workout. Four times in the barn and two times in the ring, Duke says, "No pain, no pain, no pain!" I don't think it's a denial of the excruciating pain that Rocky is inflicting on himself; it's a reminder that there is purpose beyond the pain. There is victory on the other side.

You can get through just about anything if there is a light at the end of the tunnel. And for a follower of Christ, there always is. But here's my caution: *don't be so focused on getting out of difficult circumstances that you don't get anything out of them.* Sometimes the circumstances we're trying to change are the very circumstances God is using to change us. So before you take a painkiller, listen carefully to what God is saying during the tough times.

That brings us back to Job and a few overarching lessons.

First, *let's not pretend that pain doesn't exist.* Whatever you do, don't fake it to make it. That doesn't do anybody any favors. It's okay to not be okay! That admission is the first step in the healing process. Generally speaking, Americans aren't good at sackcloth and ashes. But there is an appropriate time to tear your robe in grief, shave your head, and fall to the ground in worship.[10] When we fail to grieve, wounds remain open. Grieving is part of the healing process. It's an emotional antiseptic that cleans the wound. And different people grieve in different ways, so please give others a little latitude.

Second, *let's not explain pain away with trite truisms.* It's worth noting that Job's friends were a great comfort to him as long as they kept their mouths shut. When someone is suffering or grieving, we feel pressure to say the right words. My advice? Say less and listen more. You can say a lot by saying little.

Dark Night

Mother Teresa devoted her life to loving the sick, the poor, and the dying in the slums of Calcutta, India. In 1979 she was awarded the Nobel Peace Prize. In 2003 she was beatified by the Catholic Church. With those kind of accolades, it's easy to think of her as existing in a category by herself: beyond doubt, beyond discouragement. But Mother Teresa's private diaries tell a different story. She wrote, "I am told God lives in me—and yet the reality of darkness and coldness and emptiness is so great that nothing touches my soul."[11]

That sounds a little like Job, doesn't it?

Even Jesus said, "My God, my God, why have you forsaken me?"[12] When Jesus was on the cross, he felt farthest from the heavenly Father, yet that is when He was closest to accomplishing God's purposes. We shouldn't be deceived. When it seems as if God is letting us down, He is setting us up for something that may be beyond our ability to comprehend at the present moment.

I don't know if this is heartening or disheartening; maybe it's a little bit of both. If Mother Teresa wasn't immune to dark nights of the soul, we probably won't be either. Since Jesus had moments when the Father felt distant, we probably will too. May I offer a reminder? Faith isn't flying above the storm; it's weathering the storm. It's trusting God's heart even when we can't see His hand. It's understanding that sometimes the obstacle is the way!

If you want to know where God will use you, you need look no further than your pain. We help others in the places where we've been hurt. Our trials become our platforms. And our weakness is actually our strength because that's where God's power is made perfect.[13]

If Job endured "long and weary nights" and "months of frustration,"[14] there's a good chance we will too. But like him, we can come out on the other side more blessed than before.

The LORD blessed the latter part of Job's life more than the former part.[15]

Can I be so bold as to believe that for you and me?

I can't promise our lives will be pain-free, and I wouldn't promise it if I could. But I can promise that He who began a good work is going to carry it to completion.[16] I can also promise that in His presence is fullness of joy.[17] But our spiritual journeys are anything but linear. They are full of zigs and zags, ups and downs. And it's often two steps forward, one step back. Yet God never stops loving us through every season of life.

God is working out His plan, whether we know it or not. But we have to work out our salvation "with fear and trembling."[18] And by "work out," I'm thinking Rocky Balboa in Russia. God's gifts are free, but they aren't easy. The Promised Land was God's gift to His chosen people, but they still had to fight giants to take the land. You will too. And like them, you'll acquire some battle scars.

Pain is part of the curse, but that doesn't mean God can't redeem it, recycle it, and speak through it. It's a difficult language to discern, no doubt. But like every other language, it's a love language. And we dare not forget that we have a suffering Savior, who endured the cross for the joy that was set before Him.[19]

Pain in pursuit of a godly goal is endurable, as evidenced by the Cross. The most excruciating pain wasn't produced by a cat-o'-nine-tails[20] or seven-inch spikes;[21] it was the full weight of sin on His sinless shoulders. He who knew no sin became sin for us,[22] and one thing sustained him: you. Yes, our sin put Him there. But His love for us kept Him there. Simply put, you are worth the Cross to Christ. And if He was willing to hang on His cross, we can certainly carry ours! The Word of God chose to die the most excruciatingly painful death to whisper His love to us loud and clear.

The Shadow of Death

Congresswoman Jaime Herrera Beutler and her husband, Dan, couldn't wait to hear their baby's heartbeat. It was a routine prenatal checkup, but the look on the sonographer's face told them something was wrong, terribly wrong. That's how they discovered that their baby girl had Potter sequence, a rare disease in which a lack of amniotic fluid inhibits lung development. Jaime's baby had the most severe sort of sequence: bilateral kidney failure. Jaime was told that if she didn't terminate the pregnancy, she would miscarry, or the baby would be stillborn or would suffocate in her arms after birth.

Nothing prepares you for news like that.

What do you do when your doctor tells you that the chance of your baby surviving is zero? That your baby's disease is 100 percent fatal? That there has never been an exception to that prognosis?

While the doctor was delivering the news, Jaime felt her baby move. "To me that was a sign. I was not going to be the one to end this pregnancy," she said. Despite the 100 percent fatality rate, Dan and Jaime decided to give God the full pregnancy to perform a miracle. They also got a word from God in the Word of God.

Nothing will drop parents to their knees like a sick child, and that's precisely what happened to David after his affair with Bathsheba. He was picking up the pieces of his own shame when he got the news that his son was deathly ill. What did David do? He contended with God for the child. There isn't a happy ending to this Bible story. For seven days David put on sackcloth and didn't eat. Yet despite his best efforts, David's son died seven days later.[23]

Jaime and Dan decided to contend for their baby. In retrospect, they call it their "contending season." Their inclination was to grieve, but they fought any feeling of hopelessness. And if you find yourself in similar circumstances, I'd challenge you to follow suit. In Dan's words, "Don't rob God of the opportunity to do a miracle."

Not long after announcing that their unborn baby had Potter sequence, *USA Today* ran a feature story about the Beutlers and their baby. Rob Volmer, a public-relations professional who doesn't normally read *USA Today*, happened to spot that article in a hotel lobby while waiting for a client. The article caught Rob's attention because he and his wife had a baby with a similar syndrome whose life was saved by amnio infusions of saline.

Random, right? Wrong! God is big enough to speak through newspaper articles. He is big enough to connect complete strangers. In this instance He did both.

Rob made contact with a mutual acquaintance and then with Jaime. He put the Beutlers in touch with Dr. Jessica Bienstock, a perinatologist at Johns Hopkins Hospital in Baltimore, Maryland. Dr. Bienstock was not optimistic when she saw the first ultrasound because of the baby's apparent deformities, but one week after the initial amnio infusions, the misshapen head, clubbed feet, and tiny chest looked normal.

There was a glimmer of hope. And in Dan's words, "The difference between 0 percent hope and .00001 percent hope is enormous." For the remainder of the pregnancy, Jaime and Dan lived in the valley of the shadow of death, but they pitched their tent in the land of hope.[24] They kept contending until July 11, 2013, the day their baby girl was born, two months premature. Abigail weighed in at two pounds, twelve ounces. But she let out a cry, and you can't cry if your lungs don't work! Jaime's first thought? *That's our miracle!*[25]

Contending Season

When you get a diagnosis that is difficult to digest or a dream turns into a nightmare or your marriage is tearing apart at the seams, you have choices to make. You can stand down, or you can stand on the promises of God. You can give up by giving in to guilt or fear or anger, or you can contend by praying as though it depends completely on God and working as if it depends completely on you.

For Jaime, contending meant waking at four o'clock in the morning for trips to Baltimore for infusions, followed by long days in Congress. For Dan, contending meant putting law school on hold to manage Abigail's nightly dialysis and eventually giving her one of his kidneys.

Contending for what you believe in is harder than conceding to what you're afraid of, but it's the only option if you want to live by faith.

Where have you given up on God?

Where has hope been reduced to nothing?

That's where you need to pitch your tent in the land of hope.

That's where you need to pray the bravest prayer.

It's time to contend.

Contend for your marriage.

Contend for your children.

Contend for your health.

Contend for your dream.

Contend for your faith.

Contend for that lost friend.

Contend for that mission field.

Contending isn't easy, but here's some good news: God is contending for you! Long before you woke up this morning, the Holy Spirit was interceding for you, and long after you go to sleep tonight, He'll still be interceding for you. He contends with those who contend against us.[26] And if you are contending for a righteous cause, I promise you, God is contending for you! By faith, He fights our battles for us.

Remember the sonic shield I referenced in the very first chapter? According to the psalmist, God is singing songs of deliverance all around us all the time.[27] Think of those surround-sound songs as our first line of defense. The intercession of the Holy Spirit is the second line of defense. And there is a third line of defense: Jesus is seated at the right hand of the Father, interceding on our behalf.[28]

Quit living as if Jesus is still nailed on the cross.

The only thing nailed to the cross is our sin.[29]

Did you know that God never takes His eyes off you? Do you know why? Because you're the apple of His eye![30] Not only that, His ear is tuned to your voice, so tuned that He hears more than words.

Listen to my words, LORD;
consider my sighing.[31]

A sigh is a long, deep breath. It's a physiological response to sadness. And it's very similar to the gentle whisper of the still small voice. Sighing is what we do when we don't know what to say. But according to the psalmist, it's more than a low-frequency distress signal; it's a wordless prayer.

The death of my father-in-law, Bob Schmidgall, might rank as the greatest shock of my life. At fifty-five years of age, he was in the prime of life. He had even been given a clean bill of health by his doctor two days before the heart attack that took him home. During those days of intense grieving, I found myself sighing incessantly. That's when I happened upon three words that are some of the most comforting in all Scripture: "Consider my sighing."[32]

Even in our most profound pain, God hears us. He is so intimately tuned to us that He hears our wordless sighs. Not only that, He intercedes for us with wordless groans.[33] And that's precisely what we would hear if we could hear a little better. We'd also hear those surround-sound songs of deliverance. Just as His mercies are new every morning,[34] His loving intercessions never cease.

The Sacrifice of Praise

How did Job survive hell on earth? "He fell to the ground in worship."[35]

If you want to make it through the tough times, you have to give God the sacrifice of praise. I know that's easier said than done, but there's no other way. And the hardest praise is often the highest praise.

That's how Job survived his dark night of the soul.

That's how David survived the wilderness years.

That's what got Paul and Silas out of prison.

I have a mantra that is repeated at our church all the time: *don't let what's wrong with you keep you from worshipping what's right with God.* Don't let the voice of condemnation keep you from worshipping God; sing over it. If your worship is based on your performance, you're not really worshipping God anyway. That kind of worship is a form of self-worship because it's based on what you do rather than who God is.

The only way to drown out the pain is to sing over it. Remember the Tomatis effect? In order to sing over it, you have to hear God's whisper.

During the long recuperation after my intestines ruptured, I learned to worship God by putting a song on repeat and singing it until I believed it. There is a Darrell Evans song that I played hundreds of times. It was my soundtrack, and it eventually became my reality:

I'm trading my sickness.

I'm trading my pain.[36]

Let me make a few observations about worship.

First, *the hardest praise is the highest praise.* God loves us when we least expect it and least deserve it, but we have a hard time returning the favor. If you worship Him only when you *feel* like worshipping, you'll worship less and less. If you learn to praise Him in the toughest of times, the best is yet to come. And don't forget, you are His joy. Is He yours?

Second, *whatever you don't turn into praise turns into pain.* If you internalize pain, it only gets worse. A little offense can turn into a ton of bitterness over time, and before you know it, you're in a world of hurt. And if you complain about it, it turns into a compound fracture. The Enemy of your soul wants to keep you so bottled up that you alienate yourself from God and others. The best way to deal with pain is to verbalize it to the Lord. How? Sing over it. Sing through it.

Let me double all the way back to where we started. If your life is off-key, maybe it's because you've been deafened by the negative self-talk that doesn't let God get a word in edgewise. Maybe you've listened to the voice of shame so long that you can't believe anything else about yourself. Or maybe it's the Enemy's voice of condemnation that speaks lies about who you really are.

It's hard to hear God's voice when pain is screaming in your ear. The way you silence those voices is by singing over them.

Finally, *sing it like you believe it*. Do we really believe what we're singing? Then perhaps we should notify our faces. While we're at it, let's notify our hands and our feet too. When you're excited about something, it's not easy to stand still. I don't think you have to dance in a grove of trees like my friend Dick Eastman. But if you believe it, don't just sing it. Declare it.

Declaration of Faith

I'll never forget the song we sang the week after I prayed the bravest prayer and God healed my asthma. It's the chorus of "Great Are You, Lord" by All Sons & Daughters: "It's Your breath in our lungs so we pour out our praise."[37] I almost lost it when I sang it. Why? Because I believed it.

We don't make admissions of faith.

We make professions of it.

Steve Foster, the pitching coach for the Colorado Rockies, recently shared a story that made me laugh out loud. When he was called up to the major leagues by the Cincinnati Reds almost three decades ago, they were playing the Montreal Expos. Steve had to meet the team in Canada, but he'd never been out of the country. The customs agent asked the standard question: "Why are you here, Mr. Foster?" Steve said, "I'm here to play against the Montreal Expos." The agent didn't look convinced, because Steve was all by his lonesome. Then the agent said, "What do you have to declare?" If you've ever gone through customs, that's par for the course. But Steve had no idea what he meant. Steve said, "Pardon me?" The agent asked again, "What do you have to declare?" Steve said, "I'm proud to be an American?" Wrong answer! He was actually handcuffed and questioned, making him late to his first major league game!

Can I make a few declarations?

You aren't the mistakes you've made. You aren't the labels that have been put on you. And you aren't the lies the Enemy has tried to sell you.

You are who God says you are.

You are a child of God.

You are the apple of God's eye.

You are sought after.

You are more than a conqueror.

You are a new creation in Christ.

You are the righteousness of Christ.

One more thing. You can do all things through Christ who strengthens you.[38]

All our identity issues are fundamental misunderstandings of who God is.

Guilt issues are a misunderstanding of God's grace.

Control issues are a misunderstanding of God's sovereignty.

Anger issues are a misunderstanding of God's mercy.

Pride issues are a misunderstanding of God's greatness.

Trust issues are a misunderstanding of God's goodness.

If you struggle with any of those issues, it's time to let God be the loudest voice in your life!

THE WHISPER TEST

God is love.

—1 John 4:16

On November 1, 1937, a $60,000 grant initiated a study at Harvard University that is still active eighty years later. Two hundred sixty-eight sophomores were selected for the study, among them a twenty-year-old John F. Kennedy. Those participants have been medically examined, psychologically tested, and personally interviewed every two years since the study commenced, producing case files that are as thick as unabridged dictionaries. Those files are stored in an office suite behind Fenway Park in Boston, and as the longest-running longitudinal study on human development in history, it's the holy grail for researchers in that field.

For nearly four decades Dr. George Vaillant was the keeper of the grail. In his book *Triumphs of Experience,* he opens the vault and reveals some of the secrets. For example, the greatest predictor of happiness later in life is "warm relationships" as a child.[1] Those who enjoyed warm childhood relationships also earned, on average, $141,000 per year more than those who lacked affection as children.[2] But let me cut to the chase.

It's Vaillant's five-word summary of the study that I find most striking. He reduces that eighty-year, $20 million study down to these words: "Happiness is love. Full stop."[3] So really, it's three words! In Vaillant's words, "Happiness is only the cart; love is the horse."[4]

Hold that thought.

The Bible is a big book—sixty-six books, in fact. And as I've already noted, it was written over a span of fifteen centuries. Simply put, it is an unparalleled longitudinal study with incomparable insights into human nature and the nature of God. And although I don't want to oversimplify a very big book, I believe I can summarize the story line of Scripture in five words: *God is love. Full stop.*

The Truest Truth

There are more than four hundred names for God in Scripture. He is Wonderful Counselor, Mighty God, and Prince of Peace. He is Father, Son, and Holy Spirit. He is the way and the truth and the life.[5] He is all that and so much more than the human mind can comprehend. But if you asked me what I believe to be the truest thing about God, I would answer with the three words the apostle John used to encapsulate the Almighty: "God is love."[6]

Yes, God is powerful. Yes, God is good. Yes, God is light. But above all, God is love. That is the truest truth.

The closest I can come to explaining the heavenly Father's love for us is likening it to the love I have for my three children. I have a little saying that I've whispered in my daughter's ear since she was a little girl: "If all the girls in the world were lined up, and I could choose only one to be my daughter, I would choose you."

Is Summer perfect? About as perfect as her dad. But even on her worst day, I would take a bullet for her. Why? Because I'm her father and she's my daughter. And the same goes for my two sons. That's how I feel as an earthly father with finite love, but that isn't even a fair comparison because the heavenly Father loves us infinitely. That's a categorical difference!

In the chapter about the language of people, I prescribed the Enneagram as a way of getting to know our personality types a little better. For the record, I'm a Type Three Performer. As with every number on the Enneagram, there is an upside and a downside. My downside is that I have a difficult time comprehending that God's love isn't determined by my performance. Of course, if it were determined by my performance, that would make it about me, wouldn't it?

God doesn't love us because of who we are. God loves us because of who He is.

When we succeed, God says, "I love you."

When we fail, God says, "I love you."

When we have faith, God says, "I love you."

When we doubt, God says, "I love you."

Love is His answer to everything. Why? Because He *is* love. There is nothing you can do to make Him love you any more or any less. God loves you perfectly. He loves you eternally.

A. W. Tozer said, "What comes into our minds when we think about God is the most important thing about us."[7] If love isn't the first thing that comes to mind, we have the wrong impression of who God is. Listen closer. Sure, His love includes tough love. And we might not enjoy those "tough talks" at the time. But God always has our best interests at heart.

Remember the conference I spoke at in the UK, right after Justin Welby, the archbishop of Canterbury, spoke? After he finished speaking, Welby was asked what he believed to be the greatest challenge we face as Christ followers. Without a moment's hesitation the archbishop said, "Every Christian I meet . . . cannot quite believe that they are loved by God."[8]

Believe it or not, God loves you.

He actually likes you.

In fact, He's especially fond of you.

And that's why He whispers.

Why am I trying so hard to convince you of this fact? Because we have such a hard time believing it. Part of the problem is that God has been represented by so many people in ways that misrepresent who He really is. To those who have been on the wrong side of that situation, I'm so sorry. Please hear me: these seven languages are *love* languages!

God wants us to hear what He's saying, and we must heed His voice. But much more than that, He wants us to hear His heart. So He whispers softer and softer so that we have to get closer and closer. And when we finally get close enough, He envelops us in His arms and tells us that He loves us.

Seven Words

Mary Ann Bird was born in Brooklyn, New York, in August 1928. A severe cleft palate required seventeen surgeries, but the psychological pain it caused was far worse. Mary Ann couldn't do the simple things, such as blowing up a balloon or drinking from a water fountain. Worst of all, her classmates teased her mercilessly.[9]

Mary Ann was also deaf in one ear, so the day of the annual hearing test was her least favorite. But it was one of those least favorite days that turned into the defining day of her life. The whisper test isn't done in schools any longer, so let me explain what it entailed. A teacher would call each child to her desk and ask him or her to cover one ear. Then the teacher would whisper something like "The sky is blue" or "You have new shoes." If the student repeated the phrase successfully, he or she passed the test.

To avoid the humiliation of failing the test, Mary Ann would try to cheat by cupping her hand around her good ear so she could still hear what the teacher said. But she didn't need to the year she had Miss Leonard, the most beloved teacher in her school.

"I waited for those words," said Mary Ann, "which God must have put into her mouth, those seven words which changed my life."[10] Miss Leonard didn't choose a random phrase. Instead, she leaned across the desk, got as close as she could to Mary Ann's good ear, and whispered, "I wish you were my little girl."[11]

The heavenly Father is whispering those very same words to you right now.

He's been whispering those words since before you were born.

The Imprint

In 1973 an Austrian biologist named Konrad Lorenz won a Nobel Prize for his study of geese. In the first few days of life, goslings undergo a phenomenon called imprinting. During that process it's imprinted upon their brain whom to follow. If a bond fails to form, then the gosling doesn't know whom to follow. Worse yet, abnormal imprinting can cause it to follow the wrong voice.

Not unlike goslings, babies are imprinted by their mother's voice. The inner ear is the first sensory system to develop, becoming fully functional by the fifth month in utero. By the seventh month, a baby recognizes and responds with specific muscular movements to his or her mother's voice. Amazingly, there is no time delay between the sensory input of the mother's voice and the motor response of the baby. Neuroimaging has also shown that a mother's voice exerts a unique influence, over and above a stranger's voice, by activating the reward circuits in the brain, as well as the amygdalae, which regulate emotion.[12] Simply put, a mother's voiceprint leaves a neural fingerprint that imprints her baby's brain.

I made a bold statement at the beginning of this book: what we perceive to be relational or emotional or spiritual problems are, in fact, hearing problems. It's abnormal imprinting. We've been deafened by the voice of conformity, the voice of criticism, and the voice of condemnation, and the side effects include loneliness, shame, and anxiety.

The good news? You're imprinted by God. You not only bear His image but you know His voice. It's His voice that knit you together in your mother's womb. It's His voice that ordained all your days before one of them came to be. It's His voice that began a good work and His voice that will carry it to completion.[13]

Whether you recognize it or not, God was the first voice in your life.

Is He the loudest voice in your life?

That's the question.

The answer will determine your destiny!

Discussion Questions

Prologue—The Tomatis Effect

1. Mark writes, "Learning how to hear the voice of God is the solution to a thousand problems!" (page 2). What challenges do you have that you would welcome what God has to say about them?

2. Are you willing to pray the seven-word prayer from 1 Samuel 3:9 that can change your life: "Speak, LORD, for your servant is listening"?

Chapter 1—The Bravest Prayer

1. Why do you think God often chooses to speak to us in a whisper— rather than using His outside voice?

2. Is it relatively easy or difficult for you to hear God speaking to you? Explain.

3. Have you ever done some things prompted by the Spirit that seemed kind of crazy—maybe even to you? If so, share some examples.

4. What's your personal response to Mark's statement "Your life is too loud. Your schedule is too busy" (page 15)?

5. A verse in Scripture says, "Be still, and know that I am God" (Psalm 46:10). What role does being still play in your spiritual journey?

6. What is a brave prayer God may be asking you to pray now?

Chapter 2—The Voice

1. Mark writes, "There is one place where God finds Himself on the outside looking in, and that place is the door to your heart. If you want to hear His voice, you have to answer the knock" (page 32). Are you reluctant to open the door to God in your life?

2. How have you become aware of God's love for you? List some specific examples.

3. How would you describe the dialect God uses when speaking to you (see pages 27–28)?

4. Have you ever not wanted to hear what God might be whispering to you because you were afraid of what He might say? Why is it wrong to drown out God's whispers in our lives?

5. List the ways that God's omnipresence can influence your daily activities.

6. Are there areas of your life where you have not allowed God to be big enough to assist you?

Chapter 3—The Whispering Spot

1. Do you recall times in your life when God was "predictably unpredictable" (page 39)?

2. What role do your emotions play in your spiritual life?

3. What did Jesus mean when He said frequently, "Whoever has ears, let them hear" (Matthew 11:15)?

4. Mark describes several whispering spots where he's gone to hear God's voice more clearly (pages 45–46). Do you have a whispering spot? If not, how might you find one?

5. Do you have a unique way that you worship or communicate with God?

6. Mark writes, "Change of pace + change of place = change of perspective." Would following this advice provide a new opportunity for you to hear God's whisper?

Chapter 4—Sign Language

1. How have you experienced God speaking to you in a variety of ways?

2. What do you think Mark means when he writes, "We don't just listen with our ears. We listen with our eyes, with our hearts" (page 57)?

3. Why is discernment so important when hearing God's voice?

4. How would you explain Mark's statement "Scripture gives us guidelines, but the Holy Spirit is our Guide" (page 60)?

5. What are some examples of secondhand spirituality or spiritual codependency?

Chapter 5—The Key of Keys

1. As a follower of Jesus, why is it so important to accept the Bible as "the inspired Word of God" (page 64)?

2. What is your response to—or experience with—the following statement by Mark: "When truth is sacrificed on the altar of tolerance, it might seem as though everybody wins, but in reality everybody loses" (page 64)?

3. Famed preacher and author Charles Spurgeon wrote many years ago: "A Bible that's falling apart usually belongs to someone who isn't" (page 66). Why might that statement still be true today?

4. Why is it important to involve the Holy Spirit in your reading and study of the Bible?

5. What memories do you recall of experiencing the quickening of the Holy Spirit in your life (see page 69)?

6. In what practical ways can you abide in the Word?

Chapter 6—The Voice of Gladness

1. In your experience, do you relate to what C. S. Lewis wrote about desire: "Our Lord finds our desires not too strong, but too weak" (page 79)? Explain.

2. What would you say are the desires of your heart?

3. In what areas of your life might you be responding more to the expectations of others rather than the desires of your heart?

4. Do you feel you have found the sweet spot in your life where your gifts and desires overlap?

5. How do you experience God speaking to you through your emotions?

6. In what areas of your life have you perhaps become too normal—thus restricting the desires and freedom given to you by God?

Chapter 7—The Door to Bithynia

1. Why do you think it might be God's standard operating procedure to often provide signs *after* a decision is made or an action is taken?

2. Why does *discerning* the will of God involve much more than *doing* the will of God?

3. In your experience, how do you know when the peace of God is ruling in your heart?

4. To know God's will, which of the following tests that Mark describes—*Goose-Bump Test, Peace Test, Wise Counsel Test, Crazy Test, Released-from and Called to Test*—seem most effective (see pages 99–102)?

5. What do you think of Mark's comment that "Faith is the willingness to look foolish" (page 101)?

6. Share examples from your life of how God opens and shuts doors as a way of giving guidance.

Chapter 8—Dreamers by Day

1. How do you respond to this statement: "The size of our dreams really reveals the size of our God" (page 118)?

2. Does the Holy Spirit give you mental pictures while you are praying? What do you do with them?

3. In what ways could you increase your hunger for God (see page 126)?

4. Can you recall instances when you believe God spoke to you through your dreams?

5. What God-sized dreams has God given you? Are you remaining expectant that they will come true?

Chapter 9—Hidden Figures

1. Who are your human pinballs, the people in your life who prevent any solitary conceit or confinement on your part?

2. In like manner, who are those you can serve as one of their cloud of witnesses—people you can encourage and positively influence?

3. We all hide parts of ourselves behind a facade. What areas of your life may be concealed that God wants to heal so you can have more freedom?

4. Do you have a person in your life who has your permission to (kindly) tell you about your blind spots? Could you be that safe person for someone else?

5. Are you comfortable using your spiritual gifts or are you somewhat reluctant? Why?

6. Do you see yourself as a prophet or, at a minimum, a prophet in training (see pages 138–39)? Why or why not?

Chapter 10—The Archer's Paradox

1. Mark quotes the old adage "Timing is everything" (page 148). Can you recall an incident to two when you were exactly in the right place at the right time? Could you see God's hand in this?

2. What have been some special kairos (timeless and qualitative) moments in your life? What effect did they have on you?

3. Have you ever had a crazy prompting from the Holy Spirit? Were you able to respond? What was the outcome?

4. How might you turn up the volume of God's still small voice in your life?

5. What nudges or promptings have you been sensing from God recently?

Chapter 11—Joystick

1. How have challenging experiences in your life gotten your full attention?

2. What are things you have learned through painful experiences in your life?

3. How has pain you have experienced been used by God to help others in their pain?

4. Have you experienced a "dark night of the soul"—a time when God seemed very distant? If yes, what did you learn from that experience?

5. Why is worship such a spiritually healthy response to pain?

6. Is there a place in your life where, instead of giving up, you need to pitch a "tent of hope" in the God of miracles (see page 180)?

Epilogue—The Whisper Test

1. Mark writes, "God doesn't love us because of who we are. God loves us because of who He is" (page 187). Explain in your own words what God's love means to you.

2. What does the fact that you have been "imprinted by God" mean to you (page 189)? How might that truth change your life?

3. This book has been about God whispering in various ways. Don't forget that He whispers so that you will draw closer to Him. How is God whispering to you this very day?

Notes

Prologue: The Tomatis Effect

1. Alfred A. Tomatis, *The Conscious Ear: My Life of Transformation Through Listening* (Barrytown, NY: Station Hill, 1991), 42.
2. Alfred A. Tomatis, quoted in Don Campbell, *The Mozart Effect: Tapping the Power of Music to Heal the Body, Strengthen the Mind, and Unlock the Creative Spirit* (New York: HarperCollins, 2001), 18.
3. 1 Samuel 3:9.

Chapter 1: The Bravest Prayer

1. Maggie Koerth-Baker, "The Loudest Sound in the World Would Kill You on the Spot," FiveThirtyEight, July 7, 2016, https://fivethirtyeight.com /features/the-loudest-sound-in-the-world-would-kill-you-on-the-spot/.
2. Decibel Equivalent Table, www.decibelcar.com/menugeneric/87.html.
3. Koerth-Baker, "Loudest Sound."
4. Decibel Equivalent Table, www.decibelcar.com/menugeneric/87.html.
5. "Humpback Whales," Journey North, www.learner.org/jnorth/tm/hwhale /SingingHumpback.html.
6. "Noise Sources and Their Effects," www.chem.purdue.edu/chemsafety /Training/PPETrain/dblevels.htm.
7. Dr. Pete R. Jones, "What's the Quietest Sound a Human Can Hear? (A.k.a. '"Why Omega-3 Fatty Acids Might Not Cure Dyslexia"')," University College London, November 20, 2014, 1, www.ucl.ac.uk /~smgxprj/public/askscience_v1_8.pdf.
8. 1 Kings 19:11–12.
9. "1827. demamah," Bible Hub, http://biblehub.com/hebrew/1827.htm.
10. Psalm 107:29.
11. Mark 4:39.
12. See 1 Kings 19:11–13.
13. Oswald Chambers, *My Utmost for His Highest* (Westwood, NJ: Barbour, 1963), August 13.
14. Chambers, *My Utmost,* August 13.
15. Ephesians 3:20.

16. Gordon Hempton, "The Last Quiet Places: Silence and the Presence of Everything," interview by Krista Tippett, *On Being*, December 25, 2014, https://onbeing.org/programs/gordon-hempton-the-last-quiet-places -silence-and-the-presence-of-everything/.

17. Hempton, "Last Quiet Places."

18. Blaise Pascal, *Pensées*, trans. A. J. Krailsheimer (London: Penguin, 1995), 37.

19. Psalm 46:10.

20. "Audio Noise," WhatIs.com, http://whatis.techtarget.com/definition /audio-noise.

21. Diane Ackerman, *A Natural History of the Senses* (New York: Vintage Books, 1990), 187.

22. John Donne, "From a Sermon Preached 12 December 1626," in *John Donne: The Major Works*, ed. John Carey (New York: Oxford University Press, 1990), 373.

23. Henri J. M. Nouwen, *Life of the Beloved: Spiritual Living in a Secular World* (New York: Crossroad, 1992), 37.

24. Ella Morton, "How Long Could You Endure the World's Quietest Place?" *Slate*, May 5, 2014, www.slate.com/blogs/atlas_obscura/2014/05/05/orfield _laboratories_in_minneapolis_is_the_world_s_quietest_place.html and "The Quietest Place on Earth," www.orfieldlabs.com/pdfs/chamber.pdf.

25. Acts 17:28.

26. See Psalms 91:2; 46:1; 91:1.

27. Psalm 32:7.

28. See Isaiah 54:17.

29. Matthew Guerrieri, *The First Four Notes: Beethoven's Fifth and the Human Imagination* (New York: Vintage, 2012), 5.

30. Psalm 84:10.

31. Halvor Gregusson, "The Science Behind Task Interruption and Time Management," *Yast Blog*, www.yast.com/time_management/science-task -interruption-time-management/.

32. Mark Batterson, *The Circle Maker: Praying Circles Around Your Biggest Dreams and Greatest Fears* (Grand Rapids: Zondervan, 2016).

Chapter 2: The Voice

1. Genesis 1:3.

2. Nola Taylor Redd, "How Fast Does Light Travel? The Speed of Light," Space.com, May 22, 2012, www.space.com/15830-light-speed.html.

3. See 1 John 1:5.
4. Francesca E. Duncan et al., "The Zinc Spark Is an Inorganic Signature of Human Egg Activation," Nature.com, April 26, 2016, www.nature.com /articles/srep24737.
5. Corey S. Powell, "January 1, 1925: The Day We Discovered the Universe," *Discover,* January 2, 2017, http://blogs.discovermagazine.com/out there/2017/01/02/the-day-we-discovered-the-universe/#.WNpS1BC wRTE.
6. "Hubble Reveals Observable Universe Contains 10 Times More Galaxies Than Previously Thought," NASA, October 13, 2016, www.nasa.gov /feature/goddard/2016/hubble-reveals-observable-universe-contains -10-times-more-galaxies-than-previously-thought.
7. "Observable Universe," *Wikipedia,* https://en.wikipedia.org/wiki /Observable_universe.
8. See Exodus 14; Joshua 10; Matthew 12:9–13; Matthew 21:18–19; John 2:1–11; Luke 18:35–43; John 11:38–44.
9. See Exodus 3; Numbers 22:21–31; Matthew 2:1–11; Daniel 5; Daniel 6; Daniel 3; Mark 4:35–41.
10. 1 John 4:16.
11. Song of Songs 5:16.
12. Rabbinic tradition is not on par with Scripture, but I find it to be a beautiful backdrop and a helpful way of gaining a better understanding of the Bible.
13. Hayim Nahman Bialik and Yehoshua Hana Ravnitzky, ed. *The Book of Legends: Legends from the Talmud and Midrash,* trans. William G. Braude (New York: Schocken Books, 1992), 80.
14. See Romans 2:4.
15. Matthew 3:17, KJV.
16. Leonard Bernstein, quoted in Leonard Sweet, *Summoned to Lead* (Grand Rapids: Zondervan, 2004), 64–65.
17. Cornelius W. May, *Shh . . . Listening for God: Hearing the Sacred in the Silent* (Macedonia, OH: Xulon Press, 2011), 59.
18. Lewis Thomas, quoted in Marilyn Berger, "Lewis Thomas, Whose Essays Clarified the Mysteries of Biology, Is Dead at 80," *New York Times,* December 4, 1993, www.nytimes.com/1993/12/04/obituaries/lewis -thomas-whose-essays-clarified-the-mysteries-of-biology-is-dead-at-80 .html?pagewanted=all&mcubz=2.
19. Revelation 5:13, NLT.

20. Alfred A. Tomatis, *The Ear and the Voice* (Lanham, MD: Scarecrow, 2005), 13.

21. See Isaiah 55:12.

22. "Hearing Range," *Wikipedia,* https://en.wikipedia.org/wiki/Hearing _range.

23. 2 Peter 3:8.

24. G. K. Chesterton, *Orthodoxy* (Scotts Valley, CA: CreateSpace, 2015), 12.

25. Psalm 36:5–6, MSG.

26. See Revelation 2:17.

27. Psalm 29:4.

28. Bialik and Ravnitzky, *The Book of Legends,* 80.

29. Ed Visvanathan, *Am I a Hindu? The Hinduism Primer* (New Delhi, India: Rupa, 1993).

30. Diane Ackerman, *A Natural History of the Senses* (New York: Vintage Books, 1990), 186.

31. Alfred A. Tomatis, *The Conscious Ear: My Life of Transformation Through Listening* (Barrytown, NY: Station Hill, 1991), 72.

32. Brandon Hatmaker, *A Mile Wide: Trading a Shallow Religion for a Deeper Faith* (Nashville: Thomas Nelson, 2016), 26–27.

33. Hatmaker, *A Mile Wide,* 28.

34. I first put my faith in Christ after a Sunday night showing of this film at a church in Minneapolis.

35. See Genesis 1:2.

36. A. W. Tozer, *The Attributes of God, Volume 1 with Study Guide: A Journey into the Father's Heart* (Camp Hill, PA: WingSpread, 2007), 22.

37. Mark 7:34.

38. Tomatis, *The Conscious Ear,* 116.

39. Walker Meade, "Every Breath You Take," *Herald Tribune,* January 12, 2010, www.heraldtribune.com/news/20100112/every-breath-you-take.

40. "Bidden or Not, God Is Present," *Redondo Writer's Sacred Ordinary,* February 4, 2008, http://redondowriter.typepad.com/sacredordinary /2008/02/bidden-or-not-b.html.

41. Christopher Forbes, "Images of Christ in the Nineteenth-Century," *Magazine Antiques* 160, no. 6 (December 2001): 794.

42. "Veni Creator Spiritus," *Wikipedia,* https://en.wikipedia.org/wiki/Veni _Creator_Spiritus.

Chapter 3: The Whispering Spot

1. "Dr. William Thornton," Architect of the Capitol, www.aoc.gov/architect
   -of-the-capitol/dr-william-thornton.
2. "The First Cornerstone," Architect of the Capitol, www.aoc.gov/first
   -cornerstone.
3. "Baltimore-Washington Telegraph Line," *Wikipedia,* https://en.wikipedia
   .org/wiki/Baltimore-Washington_telegraph_line.
4. "Abraham Lincoln and the U.S. Capitol," Abraham Lincoln Online, www
   .abrahamlincolnonline.org/lincoln/sites/uscapitol.htm.
5. History Matters, http://historymatters.gmu.edu/d/5166/.
6. I fully understand that many historians take issue with the motivation
   behind Christopher Columbus's epic journey, and it's tough to discern true
   intent five hundred years after the fact. Was Columbus perfect? Far from it.
   But that doesn't change that he knelt and prayed as an act of consecration
   upon discovering the New World.
7. "Car of History Clock," Architect of the Capitol, www.aoc.gov/art/other
   /car-history-clock.
8. See Genesis 13:18.
9. See Genesis 24.
10. See Genesis 28:10–22.
11. See Exodus 3:2.
12. See Joshua 5:2–9.
13. See Judges 6:11.
14. See 1 Samuel 3.
15. See 1 Samuel 22:1.
16. See 1 Kings 18.
17. See Esther 2.
18. See Ezekiel 1:1.
19. See Daniel 6:10.
20. See Jonah 2.
21. I first discovered this story at the Hillsong Conference in New York City,
    August 3, 2016. Printed on the inside cover of the conference brochure was
    the following citation: "As told by Rev. Dr. Gordon Noyes A.C.—Wesley
    Mission."
22. Dan Graves, "John Wesley's Heart Strangely Warmed," Christianity.com,
    www.christianity.com/church/church-history/timeline/1701-1800/john
    -wesleys-heart-strangely-warmed-11630227.html.

23. Luke 24:17.
24. Luke 24:32.
25. See Colossians 3:15.
26. See Philippians 4:7 and 1 Peter 1:8, KJV.
27. Matthew 11:15.
28. See Exodus 21:2.
29. Exodus 21:6.
30. Online Etymology Dictionary, s.v. "obey," www.etymonline.com/index
    .php?term=obey.
31. José Ortega y Gasset, *Man and Crisis*, trans. Mildred Adams (New York:
    W. W. Norton, 1958), 94.
32. Diane Ackerman, *A Natural History of the Senses* (New York: Vintage
    Books, 1990), 177.
33. Ackerman, *A Natural History*, 181.
34. "Inverse Square Law, Sound," HyperPhysics, http://hyperphysics.phy-astr
    .gsu.edu/hbase/Acoustic/invsqs.html.
35. Isaiah 55:11.
36. Exodus 33:11.
37. See Numbers 13.
38. Sigurd Olson, quoted in David Hendy, *Noise: A Human History of Sound
    and Listening* (New York: Harper Collins, 2013), 20.
39. Marina Slayton and Gregory W. Slayton, *Be the Best Mom You Can Be:
    A Practical Guide to Raising Whole Children in a Broken Generation*
    (Nashville: Thomas Nelson, 2015), 166.
40. "Thomas Edison," World-Wide-Matel, http://johnsonmatel.com/blog1
    /2011/05/post_80.html.
41. Bell Homestead, www.bellhomestead.ca/Pages/default.aspx.
42. Mason Currey, "Rise and Shine: The Daily Routines of History's Most
    Creative Minds," *Guardian*, October 5, 2013, www.theguardian.com
    /science/2013/oct/05/daily-rituals-creative-minds-mason-currey.
43. Mason Currey, *Daily Rituals: How Artists Work* (New York: Knopf,
    2016), 17.
44. March 23, 2014.
45. See Acts 16:16–40.
46. See 2 Samuel 6:14–15.
47. Oswald Chambers, *My Utmost for His Highest, Classic Edition* (Grand
    Rapids: Discovery House, 2014), June 13.

Chapter 4: Sign Language

1. Charlotte Gray, *Reluctant Genius: The Passionate Life and Inventive Mind of Alexander Graham Bell* (New York: HarperCollins, 2006), 73.
2. Gray, *Reluctant Genius,* 124.
3. "The 20 Most Influential Americans of All Time," *Time,* July 24, 2012, http://newsfeed.time.com/2012/07/25/the-20-most-influential-americans-of-all-time/slide/alexander-g-bell/.
4. Gray, *Reluctant Genius,* 137–38.
5. Gray, *Reluctant Genius,* 138.
6. Gray, *Reluctant Genius,* 159.
7. Hebrews 1:1.
8. Daniel 5:25.
9. See Numbers 22.
10. John 14:6.
11. See Philippians 2:10–11.
12. Howard Gardner, *Frames of Mind: The Theory of Multiple Intelligences* (New York: Basic Books, 2011).
13. Thomas Armstrong, *Seven Kinds of Smart: Identifying and Developing Your Multiple Intelligences* (New York: Plume, 1993), 67.
14. "Zacharias Dase," *Wikipedia,* https://en.wikipedia.org/wiki/Zacharias _Dase.
15. Ken Robinson, *The Element: How Finding Your Passion Changes Everything* (New York: Penguin Books, 2009), 34.
16. See Hebrews 12:5–11.
17. Diane Ackerman, *A Natural History of the Senses* (New York: Vintage Books, 1990), 191.
18. Ackerman, *Natural History,* xviii.
19. Philip Yaffe, "The 7% Rule: Fact, Fiction, or Misunderstanding," *Ubiquity* 2011, (October 2011), http://ubiquity.acm.org/article.cfm?id =2043156.
20. 2 Timothy 3:16.
21. 1 Corinthians 2:14.
22. See Matthew 27:19.
23. See Ephesians 2:10.
24. See Proverbs 16:9.
25. See Romans 8:28.
26. See Genesis 39.

27. Alfred A. Tomatis, *The Conscious Ear: My Life of Transformation Through Listening* (Barrytown, NY: Station Hill, 1991), 70.

28. "Language Acquisition—The Basic Components of Human Language, Methods for Studying Language Acquisition, Phases in Language Development," StateUniversity.com, http://education.stateuniversity.com /pages/2153/Language-Acquisition.html.

29. "Language Acquisition," Encyclopedia.com, www.encyclopedia.com /literature-and-arts/language-linguistics-and-literary-terms/language -and-linguistics/language.

30. "Language Acquisition," Encyclopedia.com.

31. Queen, "We Will Rock You," *News of the World*, copyright © 1977, Sony/ATV Music Publishing.

Chapter 5: The Key of Keys

1. "Letter from George Washington to John Augustine Washington (July 18, 1755)," *Encyclopedia Viriginia,* www.encyclopediavirginia.org/Letter _from_George_Washington_to_John_Augustine_Washington_July_18 _1755#.

2. See John 1:14.

3. Ronald W. Clark, *Einstein: The Life and Times* (New York: Avon Books, 1971).

4. Clark, *Einstein,* 755.

5. Hebrews 4:12, ESV.

6. 2 Timothy 3:16.

7. Lawrence Kushner, *Eyes Remade for Wonder* (Woodstock, VT: Jewish Lights, 1998), 50.

8. I recognize that this is a debatable statement. There are apparent contradictions in Scripture, but in my opinion, they are resolvable in a wide variety of ways. This book doesn't provide the scope for me to give an in-depth apologetic, but I hope that skeptical readers will continue reading even if they disagree with me.

9. "Charles Haddon Spurgeon," Goodreads, www.goodreads.com/quotes /397346-a-bible-that-s-falling-apart-usually-belongs-to-someone-who ?page=3.

10. J. I. Packer, quoted in "Time with God: An Interview with J. I. Packer," *Knowing & Doing,* C. S. Lewis Institute, September 26, 2008, www .cslewisinstitute.org/webfm_send/351.

11. 1 Corinthians 8:1.

12. Luke 4:3.
13. Deuteronomy 8:3.
14. 2 Timothy 2:15, KJV.
15. Romans 8:11, KJV.
16. Joshua 1:3.
17. Psalm 119:25, KJV.
18. Matthew 27:5.
19. Luke 10:37.
20. C. S. Lewis, *A Grief Observed* (New York: HarperOne, 2001), 69.
21. See John 3:16.
22. Anna Bartlett Warner and William Batchelder Bradbury, "Jesus Loves Me," 1860.
23. Hebrews 4:12.
24. Psalm 119:11, KJV.
25. C. S. Lewis, *The Voyage of the Dawn Treader,* illus. by Chris Van Allsburg (New York: HarperCollins, 2008).
26. Philippians 4:13, NKJV.
27. 1 Corinthians 2:9–10, NLT.
28. John 1:12, NASB.
29. Genesis 1:3.
30. See Isaiah 55:11, KJV.
31. See Jeremiah 1:12.
32. John 15:7, ESV.
33. *The Physics Factbook: An Encyclopedia of Scientific Essays,* http://hyper textbook.com/facts/2004/SamanthaCharles.shtml.
34. "Alpha Wave," Wikipedia, https://en.wikipedia.org/wiki/Alpha_wave.
35. G. K. Chesterton, quoted in Dallas Willard, *The Spirit of the Disciplines: Understanding How God Changes Lives* (New York: HarperOne, 1999), 1.
36. Peter Marshall, *Mr. Jones, Meet the Master: Sermons and Prayers of Peter Marshall* (Grand Rapids: Revell, 1982), 143.

Chapter 6: The Voice of Gladness

1. Ken Robinson, "Do Schools Kill Creativity?," filmed February 2006, TED video, 19:24, www.ted.com/talks/ken_robinson_says_schools_kill _creativity.
2. Robinson, "Do Schools Kill Creativity?"
3. Robinson, "Do Schools Kill Creativity?"

4. Abraham Maslow, quoted in Jim Cathcart, *The Acorn Principle: Know Yourself, Grow Yourself* (New York: St. Martins, 1999), 115.

5. Psalm 37:4.

6. C. S. Lewis, *The Weight of Glory* (New York: HarperOne, 2001), 26.

7. Lewis, *Weight of Glory*, 26.

8. See Genesis 1:4, 10, 12, 18, 21, 25, 31.

9. Walter A. Elwell, *Evangelical Dictionary of Biblical Theology* (Grand Rapids: Baker, 1996), s.v. "good, goodness."

10. "Westminster Shorter Catechism with Proof Texts," Center for Reformed Theology and Apologetics, www.reformed.org/documents/wsc/index .html?_top=http://www.reformed.org/documents/WSC.html.

11. Matthew 6:33.

12. Philippians 3:8.

13. "Eric Liddell—Olympic Athlete and Missionary to China," January 5, 2015, http://blog.truthforlife.org/eric-liddell-olympic-athlete-and -missionary.

14. "A Short Biography of Eric H. Liddell (1902–1945)" Eric Liddell Centre, www.ericliddell.org/about-us/eric-liddell/biography/.

15. "*Chariots of Fire* Quotes," imdb.com, www.imdb.com/title/tt0082158 /quotes.

16. Psalm 16:11, ESV

17. If you haven't read John Piper's *Desiring God: Meditations of a Christian Hedonist* (New York: Multnomah, 2011), order it immediately.

18. John Piper, *Desiring God: Meditations of a Christian Hedonist* (New York: Multnomah, 2003), 10.

19. See Romans 12:2.

20. Frederick Buechner, *Wishful Thinking: A Seeker's ABC* (New York: HarperOne, 1993), 118.

21. "Passion Is More Important for Professional Success Than Talent," NoCamels, *Israeli Innovation News,* November 4, 2015, http://nocamels .com/2015/11/passion-important-for-career/.

22. Romans 12:6–8.

23. Bible Study Tools, s.v. "haplotes," www.biblestudytools.com/lexicons /greek/nas/haplotes.html.

24. Bible Study Tools, s.v. "hilarotes," www.biblestudytools.com/lexicons /greek/kjv/hilarotes.html.

25. Bible Study Tools, s.v. "spoude," www.biblestudytools.com/lexicons/greek /kjv/spoude.html.

26. "Martin Luther," Goodreads, www.goodreads.com/quotes/924405-the
-christian-shoemaker-does-his-duty-not-by-putting-little.

27. Dorothy Sayers, *Letters to a Diminished Church: Passionate Arguments for
the Relevance of Christian Doctrine* (Nashville: W Publishing, 2004), 132.

28. The Israelites failed to enter the Promised Land on their first attempt
because of a bad report by ten of the twelve spies sent to explore the land.

29. "Robert Plutchik's Wheel of Emotions," Study.com, http://study.com
/academy/lesson/robert-plutchiks-wheel-of-emotions-lesson-quiz.html.

30. "Emotion Annotation and Representation Language," https://socialselves
.files.wordpress.com/2013/03/earl.pdf.

31. Dea Birkett, "I Know Just How You Feel," *Guardian,* September 3, 2002,
www.theguardian.com/education/2002/sep/03/science.highereducation.

32. 1 Samuel 18:7.

33. Philippians 2:3.

34. "Michelangelo," Goodreads, www.goodreads.com/quotes/497577-critique
-by-creating.

35. James 4:6.

36. See Galatians 5:22–23.

37. Maria Konnikova, "The Lost Art of the Unsent Angry Letter," *New York
Times,* March 22, 2014, www.nytimes.com/2014/03/23/opinion/sunday
/the-lost-art-of-the-unsent-angry-letter.html.

38. Daniel Goleman, *Emotional Intelligence: Why It Can Matter More Than
IQ* (New York: Bantam Books, 2005), 34.

39. Daniel Goleman, "Emotional Intelligence (Goleman)," Learning Theories,
www.learning-theories.com/emotional-intelligence-goleman.html.

40. Romans 12:2.

41. Caitlin Johnson, "Cutting Through Advertising Clutter," Sunday Morning, *CBS News,* September 17, 2006, www.cbsnews.com/news/cutting
-through-advertising-clutter/.

42. Blue Letter Bible, s.v. "syschematizo," www.blueletterbible.org/lang/lexicon
/lexicon.cfm?t=kjv&strongs=g4964.

43. Kamran Abbasi, "A Riot of Divergent Thinking," *Journal of the Royal
Society of Medicine* 104, no. 10 (October 2011): 391, www.ncbi.nlm.nih
.gov/pmc/articles/PMC3184540/.

44. Journalist Malcolm Gladwell writes about this idea in his brilliant book
Outliers: The Story of Success (New York: Little, Brown, 2008), 69–90.

45. John Putzier, *Get Weird! 101 Innovative Ways to Make Your Company
a Great Place to Work* (New York: AMACOM, 2001), 7–8.

46. Luke 18:41.
47. Gordon MacKenzie, *Orbiting the Giant Hairball: A Corporate Fool's Guide to Surviving with Grace* (New York: Viking, 1996), 23.
48. MacKenzie, *Giant Hairball,* 9.
49. See Luke 4:18.
50. See 1 Corinthians 1:27.
51. 1 Peter 2:9, KJV.

Chapter 7: The Door to Bithynia

1. "Twenty Largest Earthquakes in the World," United States Geological Survey, https://earthquake.usgs.gov/earthquakes/browse/largest-world.php.
2. "The Deadliest Tsunami in History?," News, *National Geographic,* January 7, 2005, http://news.nationalgeographic.com/news/2004/12 /1227_041226_tsunami.html.
3. "Indian Ocean Tsunami: Facts and Figures," ITV Report, December 26, 2014, www.itv.com/news/2014-12-26/indian-ocean-tsunami-facts-and -figures/; "Timeline of the 2004 Indian Ocean Earthquake," *Wikipedia,* https://en.wikipedia.org/wiki/Timeline_of_the_2004_Indian_Ocean _earthquake; "11 Facts About the 2004 Indian Ocean Tsunami," DoSomething.org, www.dosomething.org/facts/11-facts-about-2004 -indian-ocean-tsunami.
4. "December 26, 2004, Sumatra Indonesia Earthquake and Tsunami," National Geophysical Data Center, www.ngdc.noaa.gov/hazardimages /event/show/51.
5. "Moken," *Wikipedia,* https://en.wikipedia.org/wiki/Moken_people.
6. Rebecca Leung, "Sea Gypsies Saw Signs in the Waves: How Moken People in Asia Saved Themselves from Deadly Tsunami," *CBS News,* March 18, 2005, 1, www.cbsnews.com/news/sea-gypsies-saw-signs-in-the-waves/.
7. Leung, "Sea Gypsies," 2.
8. Leung, "Sea Gypsies," 2.
9. Leung, "Sea Gypsies," 2.
10. "No Word for Worry," ProjectMoken.com, http://projectmoken.com/no -word-for-worry-2/.
11. See John 4:48.
12. Mark 16:20, KJV.
13. "What Does It Mean . . . ?," This Is Church.com, www.thisischurch.com /christian_teaching/celticchristianity.htm.
14. Colossians 3:15.

15. See Philippians 4:7.
16. See Proverbs 15:22.
17. "Peter Marshall: A Man Called Peter," www.kamglobal.org/Biographical Sketches/petermarshall.html.
18. Revelation 3:7.
19. Carol M. Highsmith and Ted Landphair, *Union Station: A History of Washington's Grand Terminal* (Washington, DC: Archetype, 1998), 15.
20. Acts 16:6.
21. Acts 16:9.
22. See Acts 16:11–15.
23. See Acts 27.
24. See Acts 28:7–8.
25. See Judges 6:36–40.
26. Numbers 22:28.
27. Numbers 22:29.
28. Numbers 22:30.
29. Numbers 22:32.
30. Bible Study Tools, s.v. "yarat," www.biblestudytools.com/lexicons/hebrew /nas/yarat.html.
31. See 1 Corinthians 1:27.
32. Jack Deere, *Surprised by the Voice of God: How God Speaks Today Through Prophecies, Dreams, and Visions* (Grand Rapids: Zondervan, 1996), 297.
33. Luke 22:10–12.
34. Matthew 17:27.
35. See Hebrews 13:8.
36. John 14:12.

Chapter 8: Dreamers by Day

1. "Icedream Cone," Chick-fil-A, www.chick-fil-a.com/Menu-Items /Icedream—Cone.
2. "Orchidaceae," Wikipedia, https://en.wikipedia.org/wiki/Orchidaceae.
3. Kevin Ashton, *How to Fly a Horse: The Secret History of Creation, Invention, and Discovery* (New York, Doubleday, 2015), 5.
4. Robert Krulwich, "The Little Boy Who Should've Vanished, but Didn't," Phenomena, *National Geographic*, June 16, 2015, http://phenomena .nationalgeographic.com/2015/06/16/the-little-boy-who-shouldve -vanished-but-didnt/.
5. Ashton, *How to Fly a Horse*, 2.

6. Ashton, *How to Fly a Horse,* 4.

7. Krulwich, "The Little Boy."

8. Genesis 1:3.

9. See 1 Kings 3:9.

10. Matthew 22:37.

11. See Proverbs 17:22.

12. Francis Collins spoke at the semiannual board meeting of the National Association of Evangelicals on March 9, 2017.

13. See 2 Corinthians 10:5.

14. "YWAM History," YWAM, www.ywam.org/wp/about-us/history/.

15. Loren Cunningham with Janice Rogers, *Is That Really You, God? Hearing the Voice of God* (Seattle: YWAM, 1984), 28.

16. "About Us," YWAM, www.ywam.org/wp/about-us/.

17. Acts 2:17.

18. "Toymaker's Dream Tours USSR," The Forerunner, December 1, 1988, www.forerunner.com/forerunner/X0704_Toymaker_in_USSR.html.

19. Joel Houston, "Salvation Is Here," *The I Heart Revolution: With Hearts as One,* copyright © 2004, Hillsong.

20. See James 4:2.

21. Acts 10:9–14.

22. Acts 26:19.

23. See James 5:14.

24. Bill Johnson with Jennifer Miskov, *Defining Moments: God-Encounters with Ordinary People Who Changed the World* (New Kensington, PA: Whitaker, 2016), 153–54.

25. Johnson with Miskov, *Defining Moments,* 159.

26. "A Man of Healing," Healing Rooms Ministries, healingrooms.com /?page_id=422.

Chapter 9: Hidden Figures

1. "Godspeed, John Glenn," *USA Today,* December 8, 2016, www.usatoday .com/story/news/2016/12/08/short-list-thursday/95136358/.

2. "Mercury-Atlas 6," NASA, November 20, 2006, www.nasa.gov/mission _pages/mercury/missions/friendship7.html.

3. Margot Lee Shetterly, *Hidden Figures: The American Dream and the Untold Story of the Black Women Mathematicians Who Helped Win the Space Race* (New York: William Morrow, 2016), 217.

4. "Katherine Johnson Receives Presidential Medal of Freedom," NASA, November 24, 2015, www.nasa.gov/image-feature/langley/katherine-johnson-receives-presidential-medal-of-freedom.

5. John Donne, "Meditation XVII," www.online-literature.com/donne/409/.

6. C. S. Lewis, *God in the Dock* (Grand Rapids: Eerdmans, 2014), 52.

7. Lewis, *God in the Dock,* 51–52.

8. Catherine Thimmesh, *Team Moon: How 400,000 People Landed Apollo 11 on the Moon* (New York: Houghton Mifflin, 2015).

9. Hebrews 12:1.

10. 2 Timothy 1:7, NASB.

11. 2 Timothy 1:4.

12. 1 Corinthians 16:10, NLT.

13. Bible Study Tools, s.v. "deilia," www.bibletools.org/index.cfm/fuseaction/Lexicon.show/ID/G1167/deilia.htm.

14. "Saint Timothy," *Wikipedia,* https://en.wikipedia.org/wiki/Saint_Timothy.

15. Jeremiah 1:6, NLT.

16. Jeremiah 1:7.

17. James 5:16.

18. "Henry Wadsworth Longfellow," Goodreads, www.goodreads.com/quotes/24180-if-we-could-read-the-secret-history-of-our-enemies.

19. John Calvin, quoted in Ian Cron and Suzanne Stabile, *The Road Back to You: An Enneagram Journey to Self-Discovery* (Downers Grove, IL: InterVarsity, 2016), 15.

20. Check out Marcus Buckingham and Donald O. Clifton, *Now, Discover Your Strengths* (New York: Free Press, 2001) or Tom Rath, *StrengthsFinder 2.0* (New York: Gallup, 2001).

21. Cron and Stabile, *The Road Back to You,* 31.

22. 1 Corinthians 14:29.

23. See 1 Corinthians 12:8–10.

24. Matthew 7:6, NKJV.

25. John 16:12.

26. See 1 Corinthians 14:3.

27. See Galatians 6:1.

28. Numbers 11:29.

29. Thanks to Lori Frost for this wonderful phrase and powerful principle.

30. See Ephesians 2:10.

31. Tom Kelley and David Kelley, *Creative Confidence: Unleashing the Creative Potential Within Us All* (New York: Crown Business, 2013), 56.

32. Luke 7:39.

33. "Johann Wolfgang von Goethe," Goodreads, www.goodreads.com
    /quotes/33242-if-you-treat-an-individual-as-he-is-he-will.

34. See 1 Corinthians 14:3.

35. Erwin McManus, "The Artisan Soul," YouTube video, 16:40, from a TED
    Talk given November 15, 2014, posted April 14, 2015, www.youtube.com
    /watch?v=XsJBGxmFQkU.

36. Ephesians 4:15.

37. See Luke 8:2.

38. Elise Harris, "Mary Magdalene–'Apostle to the Apostles'–Gets Upgraded
    Feast Day," Catholic News Agency, July 22, 2016, www.catholicnews
    agency.com/news/mary-magdalene-apostle-to-the-apostles-gets-upgraded
    -feast-day-77857.

39. Carlos Whittaker, *Moment Maker: You Can Live Your Life or It Will Live
    You* (Grand Rapids: Zondervan, 2013), 9.

40. Whittaker, *Moment Maker,* 10.

41. Whittaker, *Moment Maker,* 10.

42. Timothy was half Jew, half Greek.

43. It was Pastor Erwin McManus who first introduced me to this idea.

44. Amit Amin, "The Power of Positivity, in Moderation: The Losada Ratio,"
    Happier Human, http://happierhuman.com/losada-ratio/.

Chapter 10: The Archer's Paradox

1. "History Lesson 1908," Barefoot's World, www.barefootsworld.net
   /history_lesson_1908.html.

2. "List of Largest Peaceful Gatherings in History," *Wikipedia,* https://
   en.wikipedia.org/wiki/List_of_largest_peaceful_gatherings_in_history.

3. "How Much Time Does It Take for a 95 M.P.H. Fastball to Reach Home
   Plate?," Phoenix Bats, www.phoenixbats.com/baseball-bat-infographic.html.

4. David Epstein, *The Sports Gene: Inside the Science of Extraordinary
   Athletic Performance* (New York: Penguin Group, 2014), 5.

5. William Harris, "How the Physics of Baseball Works," How Stuff Works:
   Entertainment, http://entertainment.howstuffworks.com/physics-of-base
   ball3.htm.

6. Sarah Kaplan, "The Surprising Science of Why a Curveball Curves,"
   Washington Post, July 12, 2016, www.washingtonpost.com/news
   /speaking-of-science/wp/2016/07/12/the-surprising-science-of-why
   -a-curveball-curves/?utm_term=.f40dd50097be.

7. Ecclesiastes 3:1–8.

8. Isaiah 30:21.

9. Calvin Miller, *Into the Depths of God: Where Eyes See the Invisible, Ears Hear the Inaudible, and Minds Conceive the Inconceivable* (Bloomington, MN: Bethany, 2000), 50.

10. Esther 4:14.

11. "Kairos," *Wikipedia,* https://en.wikipedia.org/wiki/Kairos.

12. Psalm 90:12.

13. See Ephesians 5:16, KJV.

14. Ephesians 5:16.

15. 1 Corinthians 9:22.

16. 2 Peter 3:8.

17. See 1 Kings 11:12, 32; 15:4.

18. 2 Kings 8:19, emphasis added.

19. Esther 6:1–2.

20. "Eleven Most Impressive Libraries from the Ancient World," Online College.org, May 30, 2011, www.onlinecollege.org/2011/05/30/11 -most-impressive-libraries-from-the-ancient-world/.

21. "Congressional Record," January 3, 2017, vol. 163, no. 1, www.congress .gov/crec/2017/01/03/CREC-2017-01-03.pdf.

22. Gary Wilkerson, *David Wilkerson: The Cross, the Switchblade, and the Man Who Believed* (Grand Rapids: Zondervan, 2014), 76.

23. See Nehemiah 1:11–2:5; Acts 8:26–40; 9:10–19; 10:1–44.

24. Wilkerson, *David Wilkerson,* 35.

25. Wilkerson, *David Wilkerson,* 76.

26. Matthew 18:22, KJV.

27. Jeffry Pilcher, "Say It Again: Messages Are More Effective When Re-peated," The Financial Brand, September 23, 2014, https://thefinancial brand.com/42323/advertising-marketing-messages-effective-frequency/.

28. See 1 Samuel 3:2–10; Mark 14:72; Acts 9:1–12.

29. Acts 9:11–12.

30. Haggai 1:14.

31. William Samuelson and Richard Zeckhauser, "Status Quo Bias in Decision Making," *Journal of Risk and Uncertainty* 1 (1988): 7–59, www.hks.harvard.edu/fs/rzeckhau/SQBDM.pdf.

32. David Halpern, *Inside the Nudge Unit: How Small Changes Can Make a Big Difference* (London: WH Allen, 2015), 3–4.

33. Richard H. Thaler and Cass R. Sunstein, *Nudge: Improving Decisions About Health, Wealth, and Happiness,* rev. ed. (New York: Penguin Books, 2009), 4.

34. Thaler and Sunstein, *Nudge,* 38–39.

35. Thaler and Sunstein, *Nudge,* 39.

36. Thaler and Sunstein, *Nudge,* 3.

37. "Sex and the Single Girl," *Wikipedia,* https://en.wikipedia.org/wiki/Sex_and_the_Single_Girl.

38. Wilkerson, *David Wilkerson,* 114.

39. Wilkerson, *David Wilkerson,* 114–15.

40. Wilkerson, *David Wilkerson,* 132.

41. "The Cross and the Switchblade," *Wikipedia,* https://en.wikipedia.org/wiki/The_Cross_and_the_Switchblade.

42. "Linda Kaplan Thaler," *Wikipedia,* https://en.wikipedia.org/wiki/Linda_Kaplan_Thaler.

43. Linda Kaplan Thaler and Robin Koval, *The Power of Small: Why Little Things Make All the Difference* (New York: Broadway Books, 2009), 78.

Chapter 11: Joystick

1. Martin Pistorius, *Ghost Boy: The Miraculous Escape of a Misdiagnosed Boy Trapped Inside His Own Body* (Nashville: Thomas Nelson, 2013), 15.

2. Pistorius, *Ghost Boy,* 21.

3. "Facts and Statistics," Anxiety and Depression Association of America, www.adaa.org/about-adaa/press-room/facts-statistics.

4. See Genesis 3:16–17.

5. See Revelation 21:4.

6. Job 6:10.

7. Logos Bible Software, Job 6:10, Gesenius's Hebrew and Chaldee Lexicon to the Old Testament Scriptures.

8. C. S. Lewis, *The Problem of Pain* (New York: HarperOne, 2015), 92.

9. "No Pain, No Gain," *Wikipedia,* https://en.wikipedia.org/wiki/No_pain,_no_gain#cite_note-5.

10. See Job 1:20.

11. David Scott, "Mother Teresa's Long Dark Night," Catholic Education Resource Center, www.catholiceducation.org/en/faith-and-character/faith-and-character/mother-teresas-long-dark-night.html.

12. Matthew 27:46.

13. See 2 Corinthians 12:7–10.

14. Job 7:3, TLB.
15. Job 42:12.
16. See Philippians 1:6.
17. Psalm 16:11.
18. Philippians 2:12.
19. See Hebrews 12:2.
20. See Matthew 27:26.
21. "Jesus' Nails," All About Jesus Christ, www.allaboutjesuschrist.org/jesus
    -nails-faq.htm.
22. See 2 Corinthians 5:21.
23. See 2 Samuel 12:16–18.
24. See Acts 2:26, MSG.
25. This account was told to the author by Dan Beutler and is used with the
    Beutlers' permission.
26. See Psalm 35:1.
27. See Psalm 32:7.
28. See Romans 8:34.
29. See Colossians 2:14.
30. See Psalm 17:8.
31. Psalm 5:1, HCSB.
32. Psalm 5:1, HCSB.
33. See Romans 8:26.
34. See Lamentations 3:22–23.
35. Job 1:20.
36. Darrell Evans, "Trading My Sorrows," Integrity's Hosanna! Music, 1998.
37. Jason Ingram, David Leonard, and Leslie Jordan, "Great Are You, Lord,"
    Integrity's Alleluia! Music, 2012.
38. See John 1:12; Psalm 17:8; Luke 19:10; Romans 8:37; 2 Corinthians 5:17;
    Philippians 3:8–9; 4:13.

Epilogue: The Whisper Test

1. George Vaillant, *Triumphs of Experience: The Men of the Harvard Grant
   Study* (Cambridge, MA: Belknap Press of Harvard University Press,
   2012), 43.
2. Vaillant, *Triumphs of Experience*, 42.
3. Vaillant, *Triumphs of Experience*, 52.
4. Vaillant, *Triumphs of Experience*, 50.
5. See Isaiah 9:6; Matthew 28:19; John 14:6.

6. 1 John 4:16.
7. A. W. Tozer, *The Knowledge of the Holy* (New York: HarperOne, 1961), 1.
8. Justin Welby, "'The Only Certainty in the World Is Jesus Christ'—Archbishop Speaks at New Wine Conference," Archbishop of Canterbury, March 7, 2016, www.archbishopofcanterbury.org/articles.php/5680/the-only-certainty-in-the-world-is-jesus-christ-archbishop-speaks-at-new-wine-conference.
9. This story has been quoted and misquoted, but I believe it to be a true story based on e-mail confirmation from Bird's daughters. You can find those e-mail messages at Brian, "On Compassion: The Whisper Test," Leader Helps, February 6, 2017, http://leaderhelps.com/2017/02/06/on-compassion-the-whisper-test/.
10. Mary Ann Bird, quoted in Brian, "On Compassion."
11. Bird, quoted in Brian, "On Compassion."
12. "How a Mother's Voice Shapes Her Baby's Developing Brain," Aeon, https://aeon.co/ideas/how-a-mother-s-voice-shapes-her-baby-s-developing-brain.
13. See Psalm 139:13, 16; Philippians 1:6.

Whisper Resources for Churches

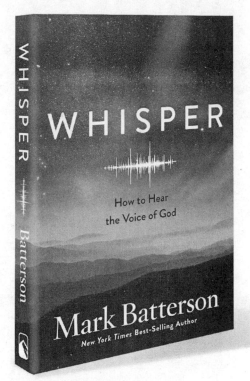

Are you a pastor or church leader? Check out these free download-able resources from Mark Batterson for leading your church through a study on hearing God's voice!

- Sermon Outline
- Video Assets
- Graphics & Shareables
- Small Group Bible Study Discussion Guide

Download these free resources for your church at MarkBatterson.com/Whisper

"*God often speaks loudest when we're quietest.*"

—MARK BATTERSON

#WHISPER

"*Speak Lord,
for your servant is listening.*"

—1 SAMUEL 3:9

Also from
Mark Batterson

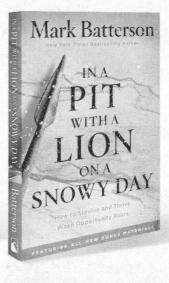

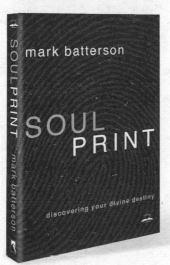

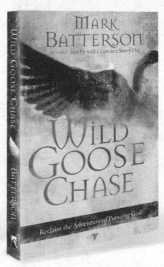